What People Are Saying About

Pagan Portals – Branwen

Profound, eloquent and passionately woven together with great consolation, *Pagan Portals – Branwen* is a wellspring of insight both into the vibrant mythology of Wales as well as the mysteries held within sorrow and grief. Kristoffer not only provides an accessible and powerful account of an enigmatic goddess but sensitively disseminates wisdom and care concerning the human condition; a guiding hand through the darkness of despair. A beautiful book perfect for those seeking guidance, solace and connection through the voice of Branwen.
Brett Hollyhead, author of Pagan Portals – *Sabrina: Discovering the Goddess of the River Severn*

A combination of personal and scholarly exploration, *Branwen: Weaver of Sorrows, Healer of Souls* by Kristoffer Hughes, focuses around the central character found within the Second Branch of the *Mabinogi*, a collection of Welsh myths. As a native Welsh speaker himself, Hughes weaves together myth and history, encouraging the reader to develop a deeper cultural awareness of Branwen's story, revealing that it is not only one of sorrow and betrayal, but also of resilience and healing. The rituals contained within this book enable the reader to connect with Branwen and provide an opportunity to embark on a personal journey of transforming grief into healing at a deeper, soul level.
Frances Billinghurst, author of *Encountering the Dark Goddess: A Journey into the Shadow Realms, Contemporary Witchcraft: Foundational Practices for a Magical Life* and *On Her Silver Rays: A Guide to the Moon, Myth and Magic*

Pagan Portals – Branwen gives readers a full understanding of this important goddess while also offering insight into Welsh paganism itself, both of which are essential. Written in an approachable style the book dives into Branwen's stories but also offers context for them and anchors them within Welsh belief, tying everything together into a whole. A lot of information packed into such a slim volume and a must read for anyone interested in Branwen specifically or Welsh paganism more generally.
Morgan Daimler, author of *Pantheon: The Irish* and *Gods and Goddesses of Ireland*

Kristoffer Hughes' *Branwen* is a deeply personal account of a deity who is rooted in Welsh mythology. He begins with an engaging story of a childhood drawing of Branwen, but this is not a nostalgic book about a figure from the past but rather a living breathing goddess who has much to say about our modern world. Rooted in a deep appreciation for myth, we learn of Branwen through the second branch to the *Mabinogi* and the *Triads of the Island of Britain*. Exploring the many facets of these stories is thrilling, bringing us closer to the heart of myth. Branwen emerges from these tales as a figure who shows us how to experience suffering, not to simply try and move on from it. Hughes takes us on a journey towards embracing personal sovereignty, and it is a journey the reader will be deeply rewarded for taking.
Andrew Anderson, author of *The Ritual of Writing, Artio and Artaois, The Magic of Cats* and *Herne the Hunter*

Pagan Portals

Branwen

Weaver of Sorrows, Healer of Souls

Pagan Portals

Branwen

Weaver of Sorrows, Healer of Souls

Kristoffer Hughes

MOON
BOOKS
London, UK
Washington, DC, USA

CollectiveInk

First published by Moon Books, 2026
Moon Books is an imprint of Collective Ink Ltd.,
Unit 11, Shepperton House, 89 Shepperton Road, London, N1 3DF
office@collectiveinkbooks.com
www.collectiveinkbooks.com
www.moon-books.net

For distributor details and how to order please visit the 'Ordering' section on our website.

ISBN: 978 1 80341 830 8
978 1 80695 054 6 (ebook)
Library of Congress Control Number: 2025950965

A CIP catalogue record for this book is available from the British Library.

Design: Lapiz Digital Services

UK: Printed and bound by CPI Group (UK) Ltd, Croydon, CR0 4YY
US: Printed and bound by Thomson-Shore, 7300 West Joy Road, Dexter, MI 48130

The manufacturer's authorised representative in the EU for product safety is:
eucomply OÜ - Pärnu mnt 139b-14, 11317 Tallinn, Estonia, hello@eucompliancepartner.com, www.eucompliancepartner.com

Table of Contents

Acknowledgements

Gyda diolch dwfn o waelod y galon i ysbryd y chwedlau sydd yn parhau i anadlu hyd heddiw, ac yn ein galw i gofio. I ysbryd yr ynys sydd yn fy nghynnal – Ynys Môn – cartref cysygredig y Derwyddon, lle mae'r hen ganeuon yn dal i sibrwd trwy'r gwynt ar tonnau. Ac i aeolodau Urdd Derwyddon Môn, fy nghyfeillion ffyddlon ar y llwybr hwn, ac i ddiolch iddynt am eu cefnogaeth parhaus, eu doethineb, a'u hymrwymiad i gadw'r traddodiadau hyn yn fyw ac yn ddisglair. I fy nghyndeidiau a mamau, am eu geiriau, eu caneuon sydd yn dal i ymestyn ac i ysbrydoli. Boed i'r gwaith hwn wasanaethu'r Awen, ac i'r geiriau yma fod yn offrwm i'r hen chwedlau sydd yn parhau i ganu trwy ni gyd. Diolch.

With deep gratitude from the bottom of my heart to the spirit of the legends that continue to breathe to this day, and call us to remember. To the spirit of the island that sustains me – Anglesey – the sacred home of the Druids, where the old songs still whisper through the wind and waves. And to the members of the Anglesey Druid Order, my faithful companions on this path, and to thank them for their continued support, their wisdom, and their commitment to keeping these traditions alive and bright. To my forefathers and mothers, for their words, their songs that still stretch and inspire. May this work serve the Awen, and may these words be an offering to the old legends that continue to sing through us all. Thank you.

Introduction

My own journey of exploring the nature of Branwen and developing a connection with her reaches back into my childhood. I was born and raised in the mountains and on the islands of Northwest Wales. My home for most of my life has been the small island of Môn (Anglesey). Once an important and significant location in the history of British Druids and Druidry. By influence of this history and richness of culture, I took to following a Druidic path in the exploration of my own spirituality and identify as a Druid. My first language is Cymraeg (Welsh), and this is important not only to my own identity, but also to the writing of this book. Language is a transmitter of culture, it is a storehouse for the soul of a people, a repository of wisdom and knowledge. It is the Welsh language that served to ensure the continuation of Branwen, offering her and her myth as a gift to the wider world.

My first interaction with Branwen occurred in my early school years, when a teacher told us her myth and in turn asked us to illustrate something from the story that pressed upon us. I recall drawing a figure of a young woman with a rather disproportionate Starling standing on her outstretched hand. I found this drawing decades later, and it struck me that at that moment in time that I had no idea or sense that Branwen would play a significant role in my future. But she was there, whispering from the stories of the past, timeless, ageless and enduring.

Branwen and the mythological landscape of Wales is a matter particularly close to my heart and my life as a Welsh person living on the Isle of Anglesey, the ancient stronghold of the British Druids. The very air heaves with the echoes of myth and the songs of the ancient, the landscape itself sings her story, bringing it to life in those who pilgrimage to the sacred sites that are evocative of this modern goddess. Living within a sacred and mythological landscape is something that I have never taken for granted, whilst simultaneously I feel incredibly privileged to have been born into a culture that is decorated with myth and to have the ability to visit the real-world places that inspired these ancient stories. It is from this perspective of cultural immersion that I offer this work as a gift to you, and to honour the mythical figures that populate my culture and my landscape.

It always strikes me as wondrous to travel to distant shores and meet people who are not only familiar with the myths that have served to preserve what are now pagan deities, but to witness people who are in relationship with these enigmatic figures. It is remarkable that what were once figures confined to the western flanks of the British Isles have become global influences in the rise and popularity of contemporary Western Paganism.

This book is the result of relationship, and I hope that the quality and depth of that relationship will be evident to you, the reader. Branwen has occupied a special place in my own spiritual exploration in addition to her cultural significance to my people, and it is this that I hope to share with you in the pages that follow. An opportunity to learn, explore and develop a meaningful relationship with Branwen from the experience of someone who has lived within the culture that gave rise to her expansive reach.

When I first began this journey with Branwen, I could not have anticipated where it would lead. This book is the result of years of personal exploration and devotion, a weaving together of culture, spirituality, and mythology that has profoundly shaped my life. Branwen, the radiant daughter of Llŷr, has emerged for me not just as a figure of legend from the Second Branch of the *Mabinogi,* but as a living presence: a goddess whose timeless wisdom and enduring grace resonate deeply in the heart of contemporary life.

Why Write a Book About Branwen?

Essentially this is a book that arose from a simple yet loaded question, who is Branwen? In essence this book serves to answer that question, but it does so from a platform of relationality. It can be said that the various deities that populate modern Paganism can speak of different things to different peoples, and yet at the very heart of so many of these figures lies a quality that cannot be separated from the mythical and cultural aspect of their being. I shall serve to explore these, not only from a cultural perspective but also from a deeply personal one. How I have connected to Branwen over the last several decades have become profoundly meaningful to me and to my life. By sharing these words, my hope is that they will inspire you to find a way to find meaning and value and reciprocation in your own relationship with Branwen.

As a native Welsh person, I carry an intrinsic relationship to the myths and stories of my homeland. These tales, passed down through centuries, are not just distant echoes from the past; they are vibrant threads of identity and culture that shape who we are today as a people. Branwen's story is one of these threads, a tale of love, loss, resilience, personal sovereignty and healing that speaks directly to the human experience. It is a tale of sovereignty and the power and loss of personal sovereignty and its implications. But beyond this cultural connection, I have come to know Branwen as a living goddess, one who reaches out across the ages to touch the hearts of those willing to listen and move into relationship with her. This book is an offering, born of that connection, to help others discover and nurture their own unique relationship with her.

My professional background has been in service to the dead and the bereaved. I have worked with the bereaved my entire adult life, and Branwen has been a vital element of my spirituality, enabling me to identify with deep grief and loss while helping me make sense of these emotions in my own life. Working with spiritual components in this way has made me a better bereavement and mortuary officer. This is the power that deities like Branwen hold in the apparent world, they help us shift our perspective of loss and grief, allowing us to assimilate these experiences into the fabric of our lives. Branwen is a powerful figure who helps us make sense of feelings of loss. Not in a way that seeks to vanquish them, but in a manner that encourages meaningful integration. Through her, we are reminded that grief is not something to overcome but something to carry forward, transforming it into a source of strength and wisdom that sits in accordance with our self-sovereignty. Feelings of grief and loss and of their emotional relocation is a difficult path to traverse, and yet it is something that we all have in common, to have non-human beings to assist us with making sense of these emotions has been enormously helpful in my own life and I hope in the lives of those I have had professional contact with.

Whilst myths can often be perceived as relics of the past, this is not just a book about the past. While Branwen's roots are firmly planted in the rich soil of Welsh mythology, her branches reach outward and upward, bearing fruit in the here and now. She is a goddess of immanence, a presence that permeates our everyday lives and invites us to engage with her as we are, where we are right now. This book seeks to bridge the gap between the ancient and the contemporary, offering both a foundation in the traditional story of Branwen and practical guidance for connecting with her in meaningful, transformative ways today. Whilst it is tempting to consider that these figures from the deep past are relics of a bygone age, this assumption would be missing the point, for these are timeless beings not limited or restricted to the passing of time. Branwen is imminently present, a force and a power waiting in the wings of myth to become apparent in your life. Branwen is more than a figure from myth; she is a presence that calls to us through the ages, inviting us to explore the depths of our own hearts. Her story reminds us that even during sorrow, there is hope. Even in the face of loss, there can be healing. And even in the darkest moments of life, there is light. It is my hope that this book will help you hear her call and step into a deeper relationship with her, bringing her timeless grace and wisdom into your own life.

An internet search on Branwen will result in references to the mythical sagas of Wales in the form of the *Mabinogi,* and particularly its Second Branch. For those unfamiliar with the Second Branch of the *Mabinogi,* Branwen's tale is one of profound sorrow and redemption. Her story is a microcosm of the human condition, exploring themes of heartbreak, betrayal, and the enduring power of compassion and forgiveness. She is a figure who knows the depths of grief and the transformative power of healing. Her experiences resonate with the universal struggles of loss and love, making her a deeply relatable and accessible deity for those seeking guidance in navigating life's challenges.

This book has been written with the aim of providing a map for those who wish to walk the path of connection with Branwen. It is a guide to understanding her story, her significance, and her potential as a goddess to inspire, heal, and transform. But more than that, it is an invitation to step into relationship with her. Through rituals, meditations, and reflective practices, I hope to provide you with the tools to make Branwen's presence a tangible and meaningful part of your life.

To that end, the chapters that follow will move between the past and the present, offering both a deep dive into Branwen's mythological origins and practical suggestions for creating rituals and practices in her honour. While the historical and cultural background is important, this book is ultimately about connection, about finding ways to bring the ageless wisdom of Branwen into your own life. Whether you are encountering her for the first time or deepening an existing relationship, this book is meant to be a companion on your journey.

By examining Branwen's mythological roots, her role as a modern goddess, and her relevance to those who seek meaning in loss, grief, and the search for personal sovereignty. Branwen is not just a character in an ancient text; she is a symbol, a guide, and a reminder of the resilience found in the face of sorrow. Through her story, we will explore how myth connects us to universal truths, offering insights into the human condition and practical ways to navigate life's greatest challenges. In doing so, we honour Branwen's legacy, ensuring that her name and story remain alive in the hearts of those who call upon her wisdom. This approach provides a balanced entry into the book, establishing Branwen's significance in Welsh culture while inviting readers to engage with her story as a source of personal meaning. This approach balances the mythological and modern aspects of Branwen in a manner that can be utilised by contemporary polytheists.

And with that bring said, let us begin our journey to discover Branwen, weaver of sorrows, healer of souls.

Chapter One

The Search for Branwen

Her name carries the weight of centuries, evoking images of sorrow, resilience, and transformation. But who is she? At first glance, Branwen is a figure from the ancient Welsh mythological text known as the *Mabinogi,* which we will explore in greater depth later. Yet, she is so much more than a character in a story. Branwen is the sister of Brân the Blessed,[1] the High King of Britain, and the calumniated wife of Matholwch, King of Ireland. Her story is one of betrayal, endurance, and loss, woven primarily into the Second Branch of the *Mabinogi,* one of the most significant cycles of Celtic mythology.Branwen's tale does not stand alone or within a vacuum; it is part of the rich tapestry of Welsh myth, a cultural treasure that has preserved the values, struggles, and aspirations of the Welsh people. Through these myths, we glimpse the worldview of early Celtic societies, their reverence for kinship, sovereignty, and the cycles of life and death. Branwen's story resonates deeply with universal human experiences, transcending time and culture to speak to us even today.

The Structure of Welsh Mythology

The primary source of information regarding Branwen is to be found in a collection of 11 native tales from Wales collectively titled *Y Mabinogion*. The 11 tales contain subcategories of interwoven myths that express the cultural narrative richness of the Welsh. Whilst centuries older than their seminal penning on parchment in the medieval period, they are reflective of an older era of Welsh history, having been syncretically absorbed into medieval Christian culture, and yet on deep diving into the material it is evident that certain themes within the myths predate the medieval era in which they were collated and collected into influential manuscripts. The primary manuscripts of note are:

Llyfr Coch Hergest (The Red Book of Hergest, circa 1382CE)
Llyfr Gwyn Rhydderch (The White book of Rhydderch, circa 1350CE)

Our attention is drawn to a subcategory of the *Mabinogion* called *Pedeir Ceinc Y Mabinogi* (The Four Branches of the *Mabinogi*), of which pertinent to this book the Second Branch will be our focus. However, an overview of the Four Branches in totality is relevant to this study.

First Branch: Pwyll, Prince of Dyfed

Key Characters: Pwyll, Rhiannon, Arawn, Pryderi.

Pwyll, Prince of Dyfed is compelled to go hunting in a forest, he sets his hounds upon a stag that has been brought down by another pack of dogs, in doing so he accidentally offends Arawn, a King of the Otherworld (Annwfn), but redeems himself by defeating Arawn's enemy and ruling Annwfn for a year. He later wins the mysterious and powerful Rhiannon as his wife, despite opposition. Rhiannon is falsely accused of killing their baby (Pryderi), who has been taken by supernatural forces and raised elsewhere. Rhiannon is punished by being forced to act as a horse and carry visitors to the palace on her back. Pryderi is eventually restored, and the story ends with justice and reconciliation.

The themes of the First Branch express, honour, identity, the Otherworld, truth vs. deception.

Second Branch: Branwen, Daughter of Llŷr

Key Characters: Branwen, Brân (Bendigeidfran), Efnisien, Matholwch, Manawydan.

Branwen, sister of Brân the Blessed (a giant and king of Britain), is married to Matholwch, the Irish king, to secure peace. Efnisien, Branwen's half-brother having not been consulted of his sister's marriage, insults Matholwch and mutilates the King's horses, leading to strained relations between the two nations. Branwen is taken to Ireland, where she is mistreated by the King and the palace staff; she sends a message to her brother by training a starling to carry a secret note. A brutal war follows. Brân is mortally wounded but instructs his men to cut off his head and return it to Britain. Only a few survivors remain, including Manawydan and Pryderi who reside on a magical island for 80 years. Ireland is left devastated by war, leaving only five pregnant women to repopulate. Branwen's heart breaks and she dies on the banks of the Alaw River on Anglesey.

The themes of the Second Branch express, betrayal, war and loss, grief, sacrifice, sibling loyalty and sovereignty.

Third Branch: Manawydan, Son of Llŷr

Key Characters: Manawydan, Pryderi, Rhiannon, Cigfa, Llwyd ap Cil Coed.

After the seven survivors of the Second Branch bury Brân's head in London, Manawydan returns to Dyfed with Pryderi, son of Rhiannon and Pwyll, and marries Cigfa. A magical curse leaves Dyfed desolate and empty of people and animals. Manawydan and Pryderi try to earn a living in England, facing hostility each time and forced to return to Dyfed. A magical fort appears one day within which hangs a cauldron. Pryderi and Rhiannon disappear due to the enchantment within the fort. Manawydan eventually uncovers the source, the enchanter Llwyd ap Cil Coed, who seeks revenge for events in the First Branch. The curse is lifted after Manawydan cleverly negotiates for their release.

The themes of the Third Branch express, enchantment, perseverance, wisdom over force, consequences of past actions.

Fourth Branch: Math, Son of Mathonwy

Key Characters: Math, Gwydion, Aranrhod,
Lleu Llaw Gyffes, Blodeuwedd.

Math must keep his feet in a virgin's lap unless at war. When his niece Aranrhod is dishonoured, her magical children are born in strange ways. Gwydion, her brother, uses trickery and magic to raise her son, Lleu Llaw Gyffes, who is denied a name, weapons, and a wife. Gwydion circumvents all curses and consequently Lleu is named, armed, and given a wife, Blodeuedd (of flowers), a woman made by the magic of Math and Gwydion from three flowers. Blodeuedd betrays Lleu and conspires with her lover to kill him. Lleu survives and is restored; Blodeuedd is transformed into an owl as punishment and subsequently called Blodeuwedd (flower face).

The themes of the Fourth Branch express magic and transformation, betrayal, identity, initiation and deep mystery.

The term *Mabinogion* whilst now an accepted title for the collection is an error due to an incorrect conclusion by Lady Charlotte Guest who provided and early English translation of the myths in the 19th century. It is assumed that the error arose from her presuming that *Mabinogi* was singular, and *Mabinogion* would be the pleural rendition.[2] Whilst erroneous, the term has subsequently stuck and become accepted as a term for the collection in its entirety. However, *Mabinogion* is not found within any of the texts, except for a scribal error in the First Branch which may have influenced Guest's conclusion. The category of Four Branches of the *Mabinogi* is given specifically to four myths that end with the statement

> *"Ac yuelly y teruyna y gainc hon or Mabinogi."*
> ("And thus ends this Branch of the *Mabinogi*.")

Later scholars were to identify this collection as interwoven myths with various subcategories to consist of 11 native tales that comprise the *Mabinogion* collection. Evidence from the Welsh Bardic Tradition, some of which are recorded on parchment centuries before the Red and White Books were penned, make several references to the themes within the *Mabinogion*. This provides a valuable clue that the tales were known in the popular imagination of the Welsh long before their Medieval incarnations. In a logocentric world, it is easy to assume that prior to their penning in the medieval era that these tales were indicative of that era alone, this would be erroneous and dismiss the rich tradition of storytelling that was prevalent in Wales for centuries before their literal iterations came into being.

Other primary sources for Branwen can be found in the collection *Trioedd Ynys Prydein* (The Triads of the Islands of Britain). Compiled some time earlier than the manuscripts described above, they contain many themes that are intimately connected to the *Mabinogi*. A further analysis of these sources will form part of the various explorations contained within this book.

The Power of Myth

Mythology is far more than a collection of old stories, it is the dreaming of the land itself, the soul's memory written in symbol and song. While myths are often dismissed as relics of an ancient world, their true function is anything but obsolete.

They are living vessels of truth, continuously shaping and reshaping themselves to speak to the hearts of those who listen. Myths do not simply tell us what happened; they reveal what always happens, they contain eternal and archetypal patterns and deep truths about the human condition that transcend the linear and sequential nature of history.

Unlike the histories written by the victors, accounts that often erase, distort, and impose; myths speak from the ground up, they reflect a history of the heart of a people in love with the land. They are rooted in the soil, in the rivers, in the breath of the people who lived in close relationship with the earth. They preserve a different kind of history, one that reflects the psyche, the soul, and the dreaming of a people in communion with the land. This is why myth often stands in defiant contrast to the narratives of conquest and colonization, for they speak on behalf of those whose voices were not preserved in chronicles or kings' accounts, but whose spirits echo through the stories passed from hearth to hearth, generation to generation.

The enduring nature of myths lies in their paradoxes, they are stories that never happened, and yet they happen all the time. They are fictions that hold emergent truths, truths not constrained by empirical fact, but truths of emotion, psyche, spirit, and meaning. Myth is a kind of magic, an alchemical mirror that reveals not only who we are, but who we are becoming. Their images and archetypes, whether gods, giants, sacred animals, or other worlds, are metaphors that speak across time, allowing ancient voices to whisper directly to the modern soul. In this manner myths are simultaneously ancient and timeless. They are immanent and imminent. They have a potential power to reach through the mists of time and be relevant to any people occupying any time of the human story. In this way, myth bridges the chasm of time, making time itself seem irrelevant to the power that they contain. Though their surface details may be clothed in the garments of Welsh

Christian culture, or medieval Kings and Queens, the themes they carry, loss, longing, transformation, betrayal, sacrifice, renewal to name but a few, are profoundly human and timeless. Their forms may change, but their essence remains the same, this is the magic of myth. Myths are constantly reborn in literature, film, art, and ritual, because humanity continues to seek ways to tell the stories that most need to be heard. We are compelled to keep telling these tales, and we can see their themes reflected in modern storytelling like *The Wizard of Oz*, *Star Wars*, *Frozen*.

It can be said that myths are the songs the land sings. They emerge from the earth herself, from her rhythms, her cycles, her beauty and pain. Humans, in turn, have listened to those songs and shaped them into stories, encoding their insights, griefs, hopes, and revelations. This is why myths across cultures often echo one another, not because they were copied, but because they emerged from the same deep relationship between people and place, between soul and soil. These recurring international motifs speak to a universal mystery about what it means to be human in a sentient, inspirited world.

Myths are not relics of the past, but a presence in the eternal now, they are a perpetual flowing river of story and connection. They can act as profound tools of understanding, a magical current running through culture, language, land, and heart. It reminds us that we belong to something greater than ourselves, and that the story of the world is still being sung, if only we remember how to listen.

Figures like Branwen hold enduring relevance, even today. The *Mabinogi* provides fertile ground for exploring archetypes that speak to universal human experiences within the human condition. A powerful metaphor for the *Mabinogi* is to consider that the branches of that ancient tree continued to drop its fruit, their seeds growing into new saplings that contain echoes of that ancient tree in the primordial forest of the Celtic spirit. These new saplings encircle that archetypal tree, forming a grove that would eventually give rise to the nescient seeds of contemporary Celtic paganism. This book and you as its reader are not separate from that forest of myth, but rather we are an integral aspect of its living and evolving spirit.

The Cultural Domain of the Welsh People

Branwen's enduring presence in the *Mabinogi* places her firmly within the cultural heritage of Wales. Whilst composed in Middle Welsh during the medieval centuries, they are rooted in oral traditions much older. These stories have been passed down through generations, preserving the collective memory of the Welsh people. Disseminated by a cast of Welsh storytellers called *'cyfarwyddon'* (meaning those who are familiar with the craft of story), they were told, retold, refreshed and made relevant to each time and locale, their tenacity to live and evolve is indisputable and a testament to their power to move the human spirit. Today their relevance can be seen in secular Welsh culture, where iterations of the myths are continuously retold, by Bards, poets, writers and TV producers.

Language is a transmitter of culture, and whilst the *Mabinogi* was preserved by the Welsh, we do not gatekeep the material, the wisdom contained within them is universal, accessible to all who may be placed in accordance with that wisdom. However, it is important that any study of the *Mabinogi* and its characters is done so with the truth of colonisation in mind, and it is vital that we strive to decolonise the material and the language we use in reference to them; acknowledging the cultural richness from which they stemmed, and honouring the people whose stories are being told.

As we engage with the myths of Wales, tales that are rich with beauty, sorrow, enchantment, and ancestral wisdom, it is essential to acknowledge the history from which they arise. Wales is not a distant or mythic realm untouched by the world's wounds; it is a nation that has endured centuries of painful colonisation, linguistic suppression, and cultural marginalisation at the hands of dominant political forces within the United Kingdom. The Welsh language, which carries the rhythm, poetry, and soul of these stories, has been systematically undermined and denigrated. With the erosion of language, so too has the culture suffered.

It is easy, especially from outside Wales, to romanticise these tales or use them as inspiration without fully understanding the living context from which they come. Myths are not just stories to be lifted from their soil and repurposed, they are the breath and songs of a people. They carry the weight of history, the resilience of communities, and the voice of a land that still remembers.

To truly appreciate the treasures of Welsh mythology is to do so in a spirit of humility, curiosity, and reverence. This means educating oneself about the history of Wales, the impact of colonisation, and the enduring efforts to preserve the Welsh language and culture. It means listening deeply to Welsh voices, to scholars, storytellers, native speakers, and custodians of these traditions. It means recognising that while these myths are shared generously with the world, they are not universal abstractions; they are specific, rooted, and held within a cultural lineage that deserves honour.

Appreciation over appropriation means forming a relationship with the stories that is reciprocal rather than extractive and transactional. It is important in any study or work with Welsh myth that one asks not only what these myths can do for you, but what you might be able to offer in return. Support Welsh culture, language, and communities. Learn to pronounce the names with care. Explore the landscape not just as a visitor, but as someone seeking kinship. Understand that these tales have been preserved through great struggle by people whose voices have often been silenced. Understand that Welsh mythology is not a museum piece; it is a living tradition.

By approaching it with awareness and respect, we ensure that its future is rooted in integrity. In doing so, we become part of a global community of listeners and learners who honour the power of myth not as a possession, but as a shared inheritance, carried in trust and with gratitude.

The Second Branch, known as Branwen ferch Llŷr (Branwen, Daughter of Llŷr), is particularly significant. It reflects the interplay between personal tragedy and political drama, mirroring the challenges faced by a small nation navigating its identity amidst external pressures. In Branwen's suffering and eventual demise, we see echoes of Wales itself, a land that has endured conquest, division, and loss but continues to assert its sovereignty and cultural identity. Within the timeless aspect of myth, we can discover ways in which we can apply their wisdom to any era, by process of storytelling one can extrapolate meaning from what may on the surface appear to be ancient wisdoms. However, wisdom is not static, it is a living, breathing spirit that transcends the limitations of time.

Chapter 2

A Summary of the Second Branch of the Mabinogi

The Second Branch of the *Mabinogi* is a rich tale of alliances, deep betrayal, conflict, suffering and profound loss that breaks the heart. At its heart is the figure of Branwen, daughter of the sea god Llŷr. A marriage is arranged between her and Matholwch the King of Ireland but Branwen is not consulted as to her wishes. Her departure from Britain sets into motion a tragic chain of events that span kingdoms and generations, it is a blending of history and myth into a complex narrative from which several meanings and wisdoms can be gleaned.

The Marriage Alliance

The story begins in Harlech, a coastal town on the western flanks of modern Wales, here we are introduced to Bendigeidfran (Brân the Blessed), who is High King of *Ynys y Kedeirn* (The Island of the Mighty – Britain). Brân is head of the household of Llŷr, the legendary god of the sea, his family consists of his sister Branwen, his brother Manawydan and his half-brothers Efnisien and Nisien. One day thirteen ships are seen crossing the expanse of the Irish Sea. At the head of the armada is Matholwch, King of Ireland who has come to seek Branwen's hand in marriage, thus connecting the two island nations of Britain and Ireland. Brân agrees to the marriage proposal and offers Branwen's hand in matrimony to Matholwch. A great feast ensues to celebrate the union, symbolising hope for peace and future prosperity.

However, discord quickly arises when Efnisien the half-brother of Brân, Branwen and Manawydan and whose name means 'hostile enemy' is enraged that he was not consulted about the marriage. In a fit of destructive rage, Efnisien takes to mutilating Matholwch's prized horses by cutting their lips back to the teeth, cutting their eyelids back to the bone, severing their ears from their heads and cutting their tails down to their backs. This is seen as an act of profound insult and dishonour. Matholwch, who is deeply offended, considers leaving without his bride, but Brân offers reparations in the guise of replacement horses, a rod of silver as thick as a finger and as tall as a man, a plate of gold as wide as a human face and a cauldron of rebirth into which any dead warrior was placed therein would rise again on the morrow as good as new but without the ability to converse. Eventually placated, Matholwch accepts the gifts, and he and Branwen depart for Ireland.

Branwen's Betrayal and Suffering

Branwen is accepted as Queen in Ireland and the couple thrive as rulers of the kingdom, eventually she bears a son who they name Gwern. However, the Irish cannot forget nor forgive the insult that was metred to Matholwch in Britain and the insult caused to him by Efnisien. They take their resentment out on Branwen for the affront and demand that she be punished for her half-brother's insult. Matholwch under great pressure from his people succumbs and allows Branwen to be mistreated. She is stripped of her royal status and removed from the King's chambers and forced into servitude in the kitchens, every day the butcher after chopping up the meat would beat her by slapping her about the ears. This mistreatment continued for three years, with an embargo placed that anyone who crossed the sea from Wales should be imprisoned immediately lest a message be returned to Brân.

Despite her suffering, Branwen remains resilient and each day at the end of her kneading trough she trains a starling to speak, she ties a letter telling of her misfortune under the wing of the starling and instructs the bird to fly across the sea and find her brother Brân. The bird alighted on the shoulder of the King and as it ruffled its feathers the letter fell to the ground, upon learning of his sister's plight, Brân gathers an army to rescue her, leaving seven men behind to protect the island of Britain.

The Invasion of Ireland

In that time, the sea between Britain and Ireland was shallow, but no ship could contain Brân the giant, and so he waded across the sea with his minstrels and bards playing stringed instruments upon his back. His army followed behind in their ships. In Ireland, Matholwch's swine herders witnessed a peculiarity, they report to the king that a vast forest with a mountain next to it was moving across the sea. The King consults Branwen who informs them that the forest and the mountain are Brân and the armies of Britain coming to her rescue. When Matholwch learns this, he attempts to make amends

When Matholwch learns of the approaching force, he is advised that all bridges across the river Liffey should be destroyed to delay the crossing of the British army. Undeterred, Brân lays across the expanse of the river allowing his army to walk across his back. Seeing this Matholwch attempts to make recompense. He agrees to abdicate the throne in favour of Gwern, Branwen's son, hoping this will appease the British forces.

To seal the peace, Matholwch invited the Britons to a great feast in a long house built to accommodate Brân's massive form. However, the Irish planned an ambush, within the great house. They placed a peg on each of the hundred columns and hung a hide bag on each peg with an armed man concealed within each bag. Efnisien suspects that all is not as it appears; ever the disruptor his suspicions grow when he questions the Irish as to the nature of the bags which they claim only contain flour. In a brutal act of pre-emptive violence, Efnisien approaches each bag and asks what it contains, methodically he finds the head of each solider hidden within and crushes their skulls between his hand, killing each one in turn.

The Final Confrontation and the Cauldron of Rebirth

Despite this, the feast proceeds but the tension remains palpable. During the gathering Efnisien commits his final act of atrocity by throwing Gwern, the child of Branwen and Matholwch into the central fire, killing him almost at once. This final and deplorable act ignites an all-out war between the Irish and the Britons. During the ensuing slaughter the Irish employ the Cauldron of Rebirth, gifted to Matholwch by Brân to revive their slain warriors, giving the Irish an upper hand in the battle and making their armies nearly invincible. In a turn of events and an act of self-sacrifice Efnisien atones for his wrongdoings and creeps among the Irish corpses and is thrown into the Cauldron of rebirth, therein he stretches himself out so that the cauldron breaks into four pieces as does his heart. His sacrifice is a turning point for the war, but the battle leaves both sides devastated. Only seven of the Britons remained alive.

The Aftermath of War

Brân is mortally wounded in the foot by a poisoned spear. On his deathbed, he instructs his men to sever his head from his body and take it back to Britain, informing them that the head will be as good company to them as it was when attached to his body. He instructs them to feast for seven years in Harlech under the song of the Birds of Rhiannon and prophesised that for eighty years they shall stay on the island of Gwales. In time they should bury his head under the White Hill in London with its face towards France. On their return to Britain, Branwen devastated by the destruction of two the islands and overwhelmed by grief gives a mighty sigh at which her heart breaks and they bury her in a four-sided grave on the banks of the river Alaw on the island of Môn (Anglesey).

At Harlech the seven survivors and the head of Brân were regaled with food and drink and soothed by the three Birds of Rhiannon, who sang to them. At the end of the seventh year, they set out for the island of Gwales and dwelt in a great hall above the sea. Three doors could be seen within this hall, two were open and the third, which faced Cornwall, was closed and was to remain closed during their time upon the island. And here on this enchanted island they forgot their woes and the suffering of war, and the head of Brân was as good company to them as it had been when he was alive, and thus this company was called the Assembly of the Wondrous Head.

After eighty years had passed one man within that company curiously opened the door facing Cornwall, and in that instant every loss they had suffered and every ill that befallen them returned to taunt them. And so, they could not rest until the head of Brân was buried beneath the White Hill in London (now the Tower of London), and that was one of the Three Fortunate Concealments of the Island of Britain, and of the Three Unfortunate Disclosures when it was disclosed, for no oppression would every come across the sea to the island while the head was in that hiding place.

In Ireland no one was left alive except for five pregnant women hidden within a cave. Those five women at the same time gave birth to five sons, they reared those five sons until they were mature. And the five provinces of Ireland sill reflect that division to this day.

And this is how this branch of the *Mabinogi* ends, concerning the Blow to Branwen, which was one of the Three Unfortunate Blows of the Island of Britain, and the Assembly of Brân who went to Ireland to avenge the Blow of Branwen, and the Feasting at Harlech for seven years, and the Singing of the Birds of Rhiannon, and the Assembly of the Wondrous Head.

Chapter 3

The Immanency of Myth

To speak of myth is to open channels of dialogue with mystery, but before we can commence, I must reiterate that myth is simultaneously ancient and timeless, immanent and imminent. Myths reflect both the divine and our own nature, serving as mirrors to the soul. Exploring who Branwen is from a purely scholarly or academic perspective is one thing, but for the song of myth to be imminent they must be approached from a different angle, one that does not dismiss scholarly contributions but deepens their meaning within the lives of ordinary human beings.

When we ask, 'who is Branwen?' it is not easily answered by scholarly dissection alone. From that perspective she appears as a sister, a wife, a mother and a figure of intense sorrow. She will appear as a human life woman who is caught within the tides of complex political agendas that tell of family loyalty, of deep betrayal and tragedy. But to leave the question there would be doing a great disservice to the figure of Branwen and her kin, for she is simultaneously a reflection, or perhaps an echo of a mythic figure, the daughter of the sea god Llŷr, she is the weaver of sorrows and the healer of souls, and as this is a polytheistic perspective on the nature of Branwen, it is to her function as an echo of the divine that will be the primary focus. However, Branwen does not exist in a vacuum, and this discourse must also focus on other significant forces that are part and parcel of who she is.

Myths act like a jigsaw puzzle, if we remove a piece from the whole entirely, we run the risk of losing the bigger picture. To assimilate their mystery into lived wisdom we must position all the pieces, and whilst that is a task beyond the capabilities of this book, I will focus on elements of Branwen's myth that may, to the untrained eye, appear like a divergence from the focus of the book – Branwen. But I ask that you consider that to deepen our understanding of her, we must also gaze to the edges of her landscape and examine her kin and the mythic world she occupies.

Myth can be a perplexing landscape to traverse, but as polytheists we have tools at our disposal to move our experience from one of passive observation to active assimilation of their wisdom. When we consider myths as reflections of the past alone, we miss out on a cauldron of meaning and transformation available to us. Her story does not simply speak of a world of medieval storytellers, but speaks of a world that is hid within each of us, one in which the voices of grief, heartbreak and the fragile resilience of the human spirit arise. Therefore, when we speak of Branwen, we speak in two voices all at once, this mystery is mirrored in the meaning of her father's name – Llŷr, or to give his full name – Llŷr Llediaith. It is here that we begin to understand the mystery held in the power of language.

According to Celtic Scholar Rachel Bromwich, the editor and translator of the *Trioedd Ynys Prydein* (Triads of the Island of Britain), a collection of wisdom recorded in tripartite form the noun Llŷr was used by the ancient poets to mean the sea, or the personification of sea. His surname – Llediaith – may have two distinct meanings, 'half speech' and 'half national'.[3] We can glean wisdom in both their literal and figurative meaning. On one level this name suggests that Llŷr was identified as someone who speaks not wholly from his own tongue, but may reflect the language of another people, it may also be indicative of a garbled and nonsensical form of speech, a common trait among European oracles like the Oracle at Delphi who spoke in gibberish, or the Welsh Awenyddion who in a trance state would spout incoherent words for the querent to decipher. This 'half speech' may only have partially conveyed and communicated truth. Bromwich also observes the notion of 'half national', implying that Llŷr is not entirely expressive of one concept of a nation, but occupies another. This may also carry the sense of a divided people, or perhaps a people who are joined with another across a particular boundary. As the god of the sea, Llŷr acts as both a connector and a divider, the sea causes the separation of nations whilst simultaneously joining them. From this perspective, the children of Llŷr are themselves figures of both division and reconciliation for they straddle certain boundaries. The nature of Llŷr tells us something important about his family and their mythical patterns, they are constantly engaged in the struggle of halves, half-truths, half-nations, half-lives. In doing so they carry within them the mystery of that which is broken and that which can be made whole again. The notion of a half-speech implies that there is a sense of incomplete or obscure conversation, when one hears only half a story, or half a truth it evokes uncertainty, to speak only half a truth is to risk miscommunication. The children of Llŷr akin to their father do not speak in clear language, instead they reflect the mystery of their origin, they do not speak whole truths and do not live whole lives, they dwell in halves.

The notion of 'half national' is equally as profound as 'half speech', the children of Llŷr are caught between two lands, the oscillation between Britain and Ireland reflects the symbolic geography of the *Mabinogi*. Nothing is as it seems, all things are presented as one half of a whole. In the Second Branch it is apparent by analysis of the Welsh Bardic Tradition that Ireland is the proxy Otherworld rather than the apparent island nation. The immanency of this mystery is profound, it implies that we too reflect this 'half national' concept, that we belong to this world and the Otherworld simultaneously. Branwen embodies this concept as someone who belongs to both nations and to neither, her fate, her destiny is bound to the sea that both connects and divides them. It reflects the very nature of our own quintessence and divine origination.

By bringing these mysteries into immanency we lift the myths from dusty parchment and into the lived experience of the polytheist and mythographer. This nuance that Llŷr and his children express speaks to the very heart of the human condition, where we might often feel fractured, divided and betwixt and between. Many will suffer from only being half-heard, half-seen and half-understood. The story of Branwen is the immanent brokenness that so many feel and the longing for wholeness, and in that longing we can reclaim our Otherworldly origin and learn that wisdom does not arise from certainty but rather from navigating that which is fractured.

Echoes of a goddess

When we speak of Branwen, we speak in two voices, the first reflected above, the second in her nature as a goddess who has continually spoken her mysteries to those who would listen. But in the same manner as her father, she speaks in half-speech, deciphering her meaning is half the battle, the other half is developing an immanent relationship with her that imminently transforms the present. Whilst we can argue as to whether Branwen was perceived as a goddess in antiquity, it is beyond the scope of this short book. That she may reflect an older mythical divinity, with suggestions of Branwen being a euhemerised deity from ancient times will be explored later in this book, but by the process of apotheosis she has risen to the needs of modern polytheists and goddess centred spirituality for her message is as necessary and essential today as it ever was.

Branwen has found a renewed life in modern times and the lived experience of those who seek to navigate divisions within their own lives, and she does so not as a figure that waves a magic wand and makes 'everything ok' but rather asks us to consider how we can reconcile the often-opposing halves of our own lives. The emphasis of responsibility is placed entirely upon us, and Branwen and her kin act as allies in our quest for wholeness.

The challenge of this book is to bring the two voices and two nations reflected in her family name together, it is both the voice of myth and the voice of an acute and lived reality. When we engage with these figures from myth we come face to face with our own lives, with the often life shattering events that tear at our own wellness, and Branwen can be there to offer a hand through the forest of being, as weaver of sorrows and healer of souls.

The following statement I present to you fully as a polytheist and not as a scholar or expert on Celtic matters, but rather as a Druid who also dwells between two realities. It is important from a polytheistic and modern pagan perspective to understand that the figures that populate the *Mabinogi* are not merely human characters but instead represent the gods and goddesses of culture that for narrative purposes are clothed as mortals. The medieval storyteller and Bards were not preserving intact gods but were weaving their stories into the very fabric of a Christian society that could no longer conceptualise them as divine. The existence of deities beyond the monotheistic norm would have been anathema to that society, instead the storytellers and Bards intricately weaved the concept of the supernatural and the echoes they contained into a new time, moving along with new ideas of spirituality and religion rather than beating the drum of worn-out Druids desperately clinging to an old world and its old ways. Just like the Welsh language, the stories and poetry evolved and developed with the people and the influences upon them.

To this day we can see the influence of the supernatural and the indigenous Otherworld – Annwfn[4] – bleeding through into medieval storytelling, not concerning itself greatly with Christian doctrine, but fusing together two halves of two stories, one foot in the Welsh Otherworld and the other in medieval Christian society. This duality, reflected in the patronym of the Children of Llŷr is crucial to the modern polytheist, whilst Branwen's story is on one hand mythic, it is also deeply human. The tale can easily be read as an epic tale of marriage and betrayal, old politics and dreadful violence, but it can also be read as a myth of divine children whose mysteries and lives reflect sovereignty, loss and the journey between worlds. Both aspects are true and necessary.

The Necessity of Myth Today

How do these myths concern us, what sense can we make of a battle between Kings and ancient nations, of medieval customs and severed heads, of the death of a child and the decimation of two countries? What can those themes possibly have to do with our own lives and living?

It is in answering these necessary questions that we move deeper into the timeless ability of myths to transform those who connect with them. For the polytheist it would be foolhardy to consider myths as historical accounts, instead myths act as mirrors to the human condition and the nature of the human soul. When we encounter Branwen's suffering, we see within her condition a reflection of all those who have ever been silenced, who have been abused, marginalised and offered up as scapegoats. In her brother's sacrifice we can see one half of the vision of death and its meaning, and the continuation of the human soul. In her half-brother's intense rage and bitterness, we can see the deep chaos that resides within us, and the path towards atonement of wrongdoings. The beauty of myth is that they continue to reflect our human experiences back to us, and this is the lesson that arises from developing a relationship with Branwen. She weaves sorrows like intricate Celtic knot-work, and in a manner of speaking we are all caught in the turning of her loom.

In the 21st Century there is a tendency in self-help and wellness circles to transcend that which blights us, but in Branwen's tale we see something quite different. Not only is this story about the downfall of dynasties, but it is also about the sovereignty of the self and the maintaining of dignity against all odds, even if the outcome is bleak. Within the pages of this myth, we see the utter shattering of an individual's life and the immense collateral damage that encircles her. She is a figure that carries the burden of sorrow until death – there is a powerful message here. Welsh myth does not sugarcoat the sorrows, it does not offer a guaranteed path to healing or reconciliation, instead it acts as a door through which we can chose to walk through or choose to close and live within the tumult of our denied destiny.

Branwen does not persist to sugarcoat the truth, she shows us that sorrow is real, and that loss and grief can tear us apart in ways that we cannot always avoid. The emphasis is on us to traverse and navigate the waves, the decision to either step into them and be reshaped and transformed or to deny them entirely and consequently live in fragments is ours alone. By denouncing the reality of our own brokenness, by crushing the loom of emotion and ignoring it we see only half-truths and live only half-lives. From the perspective of the myth it makes absolutely no difference, the stories do not care whether we follow their guidance or not, they exist as signposts along the road. They point towards the potential of living fully and authentically as us, weaving the idiosyncrasies of the human experience into the tapestry of our life's purpose. This may sound somewhat doom and gloom, but life often is, the beauty of connecting with a goddess like Branwen is the potential for healing and transformation. She can be the goddess we need to guide us to understand loss and grief, she shows us that even in sorrow there is a thread of transformation that we can then weave into our lives, she tells us that even in silence and separation there can be song. The choice is ours; the responsibility is ours, but in that responsibility lies our ability to respond which mirrors the authenticity of the self.

Death and Reconciliation in the Second Branch

The *Mabinogi of Branwen* carries another immanent and imminent message, that of death and dying. It is another important factor of the mysteries that we cannot and should not sugarcoat. When considering the myth, death is a constant presence, and it is true that not all things end well. Branwen dies. Gwern dies. Efnisien dies. Brân himself eventually dies. Death is neither avoided nor sugar-coated, it is in the nature of the myth to simply state it as it is, death happens, and that is perhaps one of the deepest lessons of the Second Branch.

There is a tendency, particularly in Western culture to avoid death at all costs, we fear it, we hide it from sight, we consider that death is the ultimate failure. In the *Mabinogi of Branwen* death and endings are woven into the very fabric of life itself. However tragic the circumstances, death is not cast as a villain or an aberration but is perceived as an integral part of the pattern. The true tragedy of Branwen's tale is not the fact that she dies, but rather that she dies of a broken heart, she carries sorrows that were never healed. This is the song that she sings, and in that singing she offers us a way to rewrite the lyrics of our own suffering.

We perceive death to be the biggest problem, we try our utmost to keep it at bay, but death has never been the problem, our fear of it is the problem. We set in motion ways in which we can close our hearts and minds to its reality, that we can somehow escape it, and in doing so we run the risk of creating half-lives, a state of fragility that break at the first touch of sorrow. Branwen and her kin do not encourage us to run from death, but to have the courage to face it with dignity, to walk through its dappled groves with wisdom and to find meaning in how we will eventually meet it.

Through the weaving of sorrows, Branwen teaches us that we cannot always mend that which is broken and that we might never regain that which is lost to us. What she offers is a different point of view, that there is also beauty and a quiet strength in facing sorrow without denial, and in doing so she facilitates a stripping away of illusion that may bind us to half-truths, leaving us with truth. Her message resounds through time, that however difficult, however triggering, truth is always more liberating than fear.

A Living Myth

So many of the themes explored above may appear distant, or even triggering, where sea gods, ravens, severed heads and death can at times be too poignant a reminder of the fragility of life. And yet, what they represent from a mythic perspective continue to impact on human life to this day. The sea still howls against the rocks of Harlech, the experience of grief, loss and betrayal is as real to us now as it was over a thousand years ago. We have changed little over that span of time. And yet the ravens of Brân still guard the Tower of London today, pearls of sovereignty can still be found in the depths of oneself. When we move into relationship with Branwen and her kin we are not working with relics of the past, but rather we move into connection with a living presence, a goddess who continues to weave her sorrows with our own. She teaches us that we are the children of the gods, that we inherited these myths from our ancestors, their mysteries live within our gweilgi. Within the drama and perplexion of myth we are invited to speak to the ancient and timeless aspect of ourselves, to speak across centuries and nations, not in half-truths or half-speech, but reflections of a deeper truth.

As we progress through this book, keep in mind the nature of the family of Llŷr, half-speech, half-national, and that you bring the third component to this mystery, the experience of your life enriches the soul of the world, contributes to the memory of the universe. To emulate the function of Llŷr and his children, the discourse of this book can be seen to contain two halves, one which expresses the need of an author to deepen your experience of a goddess, and the other which waits for you, the reader, to step into the currents of the tale and make it your own. For without your participation, the myth remains unfinished. You are the third voice that completes the half-speech, the half-national, it is your life and connection to Branwen that reveals the whole.

Chapter 4

Otherworldly Influences on the Second Branch

The tale of Branwen is a rich exploration of themes that resonate across time, and whilst this book has its primary focus on Branwen, it is important to acknowledge that she does not exist in a vacuum, and her story is intimately tied to the themes and relationships that are explored in the tale.

She forms part of a wider jigsaw puzzle that is steeped in mythological allegory combined with pseudo-historical references that may reflect events in the apparent world. It is tempting to consider the brief historical references within the Second Branch to a time just before the coming of the Romans to Britain, held in the narrative of Caradog the son of Brân, this supposition may represent a survival of the story of the British hero Caractacus son of Cunobelinus, who allegedly led the Britons, albeit unsuccessfully against Aulus Plautius in 43CE.[5] The Second Branch and the *Triads of the Island of Britain* make further references to Caswallawn the Son of Beli (Cassivellaunos) who led an army of Britons against Ceaser and his second expedition to Britain. According to Celtic Scholar Rachel Bromwich, this reference could be a medieval speculation alone or represent a genuine traditional memory of a historical British ruler.[6] Furthermore, Sir Ifor Williams in his exploration of the *Four Branches of the Mabinogi* hypothesises that the *Mabinogi* reflect a period before the Romans had fully arrived in Britain, and that in the mind of the storyteller the landscape of the *Mabinogi* is pre-Roman invasion. He further speculates that the *Mabinogi* are echoes of the pre-Christian pagan era of Britain.[7] Whilst elements of the above remarks are indicative of hypothesis and speculation, they are not wholly misinformed or assumed. In all likelihood, the *Mabinogi* do indeed contain echoes of the deep past, with syncretic overlays from the medieval period and the rich diversity of the storytelling traditions of Wales. However, regardless of the possibility of timestamps hidden within the narrative it is vitally important that the contemporary reader appreciates that we are dealing with myth, and elements of myth which are simultaneously of the past and of now. It is the timelessness of the myths that will be the primary focus of this discourse. Therefore, it is essential that we seek out the clues left by the storytelling tradition that informed the listener, or indeed the modern reader, that other forces are at work. Whilst the language of the *Mabinogi* contains overtly Christian overtones, there is little of Christan thought or doctrine found within them. Instead, they are demonstrative of supernatural themes that do not conform with Christian thinking in either its medieval or contemporary guise. It is to these themes that the modern polytheist should look to glean wisdom.

On initial examination the Second and Third Branches of the *Mabinogi* may lack the overtly magical themes of the First and Fourth Branches, but I would argue that the influences of supernature and the Otherworld are present if one knows where to look. In studying the myth, subtle clues are revealed to inform the reader of the influence of the Otherworld on the structure of the tale, these are important clues that would have been understood by the audience at the time of their telling. For a modern audience these clues can easily be overlooked as minor or insignificant narrative details, however, their inclusion is significant and intentional.

In the original manuscripts which contain the most complete versions of the *Mabinogi,* namely the *Llyfr Gwyn Rhydderch* (White Book of Rhydderch) and the *Llyfr Coch Hergest* (Red Book of Hergest), mystery is conveyed within the first paragraph that alludes to the supernatural origins and nature of the family of Llŷr, a subtlety that is lost in translation, so sayeth the manuscript:

> *Bendigeidfran fab Llŷr, a oed frenin coronawc ar yr ynys hon, ac ardyrchawc o goron Lundein. A frynhawngueith yd oed yn Harlech yn Ardudwy, yn llys idaw. Ac yn eisted yd oedynt ar garrec Hardlech, uch penn y weilgi, a Manawydan fab Llŷr y urawt y gyt ac ef, a deu froder un fam ac ef, Nissyen ac Efnyssyen, a guyrda y´am hynny, mal y gwedei ynghylch a brenhin.*[8]
>
> Bendigeidfran the son of Llŷr was crowned king over this island and invested upon him was the crown of London. One afternoon he was in Harlech, in Ardudwy, one of his courts, he was sitting on the rock of Harlech above the sea, with his brother Manawydan son of Llŷr, and his two brothers from the same mother, Nisien and Efnisien, and there were noblemen too as was customary around a king.[9]

Whilst the above common translation appears straightforward and descriptive, a significant detail is lost. I draw your attention to the original text and note the line '*Ac yn eisted yd oedynt ar garrec Hardlech, uch penn y weilgi*'. In modern translations this is translated as 'he was sitting on the rock of Harlech above the sea'. However, in the original middle Welsh the word translated to mean 'sea' is *'weilgi'*, the common term for sea in Welsh is *'môr'*, therefore, what might be the difference, is this simply an older term for 'sea'? The answer to that question belies a mystery that is indicative of the supernatural nature and origin of the family of Llŷr.

Weilgi is a mutation of *'Gweilgi'*, a mutation is a common grammatical peculiarity in the Welsh language where the initial letter of a word will either be dropped or changed to another letter depending on the sentence structure and the words preceding them. To search the dictionary for the term 'weilgi' would result only in frustration lest one knows it has been subject to mutation. The redactor, no doubt taking their lead from the cyfarwyddon (storytellers) at the time faithfully recorded the term 'weilgi', but they may have done so with little or no understanding of its ancient significance. If we search for the original word prior to mutation, it appears as 'gweilgi' which according to the *Geiriadur Prifysgol Cymru* (Dictionary of the Welsh Language) is closely related to the term *'blaidd'* meaning a wolf, or rather the sound a wolf might make, in addition the term is used to describe a form of personality that arises from the sea as a totality; or a mythological idea of an animal howling over the sea. Whilst connected to the nature of the sea, the term is correctly rendered as referring to the deep, or a flood or torrent. [10] The Welsh language is by its very nature poetic, and it is a truism that the language evolved and developed hand in hand with poetry. Poetic meaning is infused inexorably into the language; words are chosen carefully to convey a deeper significance to the narrative or poetic structure within the storytelling and Bardic tradition. The symbolic or metaphoric nuance of such terms often do not survive the mechanisms of translation. By using the mutated word 'weilgi' the redactor, and by proxy the earlier cyfarwydd, is signalling to the audience that the tale is not grounded in the mundane world, but rather in a mythological landscape. Gweilgi is not merely the sea in its apparent sense but the deep, the abyssal ocean which carries a supernatural overtone, a howling depth that lies beyond human reach and comprehension. The storyteller is deliberately situating Brân and his retinue directly in the ordinary world but on the threshold of the Otherworld. This deep is not just water in a physical sense but a liminal space where the gods, monsters and other mythic forces dwell.

In his position sitting upon the rock of Harlech he does not represent a mere monarch casually surveying his coastline, but represents a god seated at the edge of creation, gazing into the abyss from which order and sovereignty must be wrangled. Within this single term we can glean magical meaning, as is common in the *Mabinogi*, from the offset we are being introduced to an archetypal image, the ruler at the edge of chaos, the mediator between civilisation and the Otherworld, the giant whose very body becomes the bridge between realms. To a medieval audience the storyteller is whispering that they are hearing a tale of gods as opposed to mortals.

The sea refers to that which is upon the surface, visible and apparent, the gweilgi, the deep, reminds is that behind the veneer of royal politics lies a deeper mythic narrative of deities playing out a cosmic drama, one that involves sovereignty, betrayal and transformation. The gweilgi acts as a metaphor for the submerged, unseen, to hidden truths, half-remembered mysteries and mythological archetypes concealed beneath the apparent surface of the tale. When we notice this hidden meaning the tale invites us to read mythically rather than historically. For the modern polytheist this tale at its outset invites us to sit with Brân on the rock of Harlech,[11] not as students of history but as mythographers, and there to ask:

- What is the abyss that I face in my own life and living?
- What is it that roars from the deep within me?

Brân, Branwen and their family are not mortals as we would understand it, but euhemerized gods whose true nature emerges in the story's peculiar nature, its tragedy and Otherworldly symbols. Through time the story evolved by process of intense euhemerization from its mythological origin to one seemingly concerned with the actions of human Kings.[12] However, one must remember that Brân, Branwen, and their brother Manawydan are the Children of Llŷr, the sea god, this observation deepens everything that has unfolded about the gweilgi. What we see here is an echo of a myth where the sea's children are engaging with the fate of nations. Llŷr is not an ordinary progenitor but a god, and by proxy his children carry the qualities of the deep, its vastness and mystery, and its immense power to sustain and destroy.The gweilgi is not just the sea, it represents the realm of their father, Llŷr, the divine source of their entire being. Brân's gaze out to the gweilgi is on one hand a recognition of his origin and on the other a reminder that this story is not fully human but cosmic in nature. Gweilgi is figuratively used as the howling deep which reflects the presence of the divine nature of the sea itself, one that is roaring and howling behind the veil of euhemerization. The mysteries and meaning that we can be placed in accordance with are expressed through the deeper levels of this myth, Brân, Branwen and their kin represent the hidden undercurrents of the sea in a metaphoric sense, it is vast, uncontrollable, life-giving and devastating whilst also acts as a mirror for our inner depths.

As the tale unfolds from this supernatural origination, we can be placed in accordance with its wisdom by considering that Brân shows us how to bridge that which might feel unbridgeable. Branwen shows us that the tides or grief are oceanic, they cannot be fully contained, only felt and honoured. Brân and Branwen carry the mysteries of the deep and of the corvid species of birds who in turn express another wisdom, death, prophecy, grief, and the promise of transformation when we listen to the voice of the deep.

The humanisation of Brân, Branwen and Manawydan is part of the process of euhemerization where mythic figures are recast as human-like monarchs, rulers and mortals. However, we can clearly see hints of their mythic origins within the tale, albeit partially submerged by the nature of the narrative and its evolution. Brân is too large to be accommodated in a building for the sea cannot be contained by mortal means. His decapitated head continues to speak, counsel and offer wisdom for the sea god's son cannot be silenced even in death. Branwen's tragic life in Ireland mirrors the mystery of the sea which offers riches but demands loss. Her suffering and eventual return across the waters and her apparent death from heartbreak on the banks of the river Alaw on the isle of Môn are indicative of the mysteries of the deep, tides of joy and sorry, abundance and profound loss.

Hidden Power – Liminal Presence

In the scene at Harlech, which is situated on the northwestern coast of modern Wales, we are introduced to Brân and his retinue of men and nobles, but Branwen is absent, she is not mentioned until Matholwch of Ireland asks for her hand in marriage. To a modern audience this exclusion of a female figure may appear problematic or misogynistic, but this omission is not accidental nor provocative but entirely intentional. It is commonplace in medieval Welsh storytelling for women to be introduced at pivotal points and they often appear as catalysts of transformation. Branwen is not introduced to the audience as an element of static sovereignty but rather as the hinge of fate, her introduction foretells that change is about to commence. Branwen is no less or greater a divine force than her brothers, but she is veiled and concealed until the moment when her role as sovereignty goddess becomes utterly unavoidable and initiates the dynamics of the tale. Whilst on one hand her absence might be perceived as a form of ritual modesty, on the other it highlights her role as not a cog in the wheel of the stable, masculine order of Harlech but rather as a symbol for the sea of transformation that is about to engulf both nations. She is the pivotal figure whose introduction sets the entire plot into motion.

Her absence in the initial stage of the tale foreshadows her later isolation. She is a liminal figure, and the power of liminality can be seen as a common thread throughout the tale.

From the offset we are informed that Matholwch arrives in an armada of thirteen ships. This number in of itself signals a disruption to the natural order of things, thirteen lies beyond the perfection of twelve, 12 months, 12 signs of the zodiac etc. The number thirteen in European tradition disrupts the normal cycle, it signals an imbalance and transgression. His ships cross the gweilgi, indicating the arrival of an ominous and Otherworldly influence. The eventual marriage proposal and her later introduction is intentional, she is not a part of the opening scene for her destiny lies across the sea. She is being slowly drawn into the Otherworld that in the tale is represented as Ireland.

In taking the above into consideration it becomes apparent to the modern reader that significant details are omitted by process of translation, mystery hides beneath the surface of language. Common language can be perceived as the sea, that which we observe on the surface, but a unique feature of Welsh is that it contains a deeper aspect, like the gweilgi, the structure of the language and its poetic origins sing of deeper meaning. This would have been understood to a medieval audience and would have contained a deeper meaning to those privy to the secrets of the Bards and storytellers. In conclusion, these subtle layers belie a hidden meaning that informs the audience that all is not as it seems, that the influence of Otherworldly forces is at play.

The layers of complex mystery deepen as we explore the zoomorphic components of the tale.

Chapter 5

Zoomorphic Influences within the Second Branch

The native tales of the various Celtic nations explicitly explore the notion of an Otherworldly reality that frequently interacts with the apparent world. This is in stark contrast to the accepted reality and universal worldview gleaned from the revealed religion predominant in the medieval period. People can rarely conceptualise that which they have no concept of, and in the minds of medieval storytellers and audiences the notion of an Otherworld would have been anathema to Christian doctrine, hence the indigenous Otherworld of the Welsh, Annwfn, is frequently referred to as Hell, albeit its description is far removed from the concept of a place of eternal suffering and damnation.

The rationale for this is rather simple, only three realms of existence is possible in Christian doctrine, the apparent world, the heavenly otherworld of the blessed and the realm of eternal separation from the Christian God, Hell. Any realm that existed outside of this limited structure would have not been fully understood and sloppily rendered as a place where God did not dwell, hence Annwfn is referred to on numerous occasions as hell. However, within the mind of the cyfarwydd (storyteller), the Otherworld was indicative of an older, native belief in an entirely separate realm of existence that did not conform to Christian doctrine, and this romantic and contradictory notion posed a significant problem, one which was dealt with by consigning it to the worldview of Christianity, with the only viable option being Hell as opposed to Heaven.

From a folkloric perspective the notion of an indigenous Otherworld was never fully extinguished, and its presence, however enigmatic, survived and continues to survive to this day. The Bardic Tradition of Wales, containing a rich storehouse of literal works spanning over one thousand four hundred years, reflect not only socio-political development in Wales, but also socio-religious thought which express a subtle continuation of belief in an Otherworld and its forces that do not conform to Christian thinking. When reading the myths, the modern polytheist and pagan practitioner can glean significant wisdom from the clues that hint at these Otherworldly forces and when they appear in the narrative, as described in the previous chapter. Another significant clue can be found in the appearance of certain zoomorphic figures that punctuate the narrative. Their appearance can be so subtle that to a contemporary audience they are easily overlooked as insignificant, to a medieval and earlier audience and the discerning modern explorer they are indicative of forces beyond the apparent. These themes are worthy of a deeper exploration in this discourse to demonstrate the deepening influence of the Otherworld.

The significance of Corvids will warrant its own exploration which will follow this chapter, in the meantime I turn your attention to other subtle zoomorphic forces within the tale.

The theme of sovereignty is represented by the horses of Matholwch in the opening paragraphs of the Second Branch, Efnisien's brutal mutilation of the horses is a direct attack on the sovereignty that they represent. This is an important moment in the tale, and whilst it is commonly understood today that horses represent sovereignty, this understanding would have been significantly visceral to a medieval audience. The principle of sovereignty, self and otherwise is under attack, denigrated and threatened by the actions of Efnisien, from this point onwards the sovereignty of both Britain and Ireland hang in the balance. The redactor clearly plays on this dynamic and we can summarise the threats to sovereignty in the following guise:

- *The fragility of Alliances:* The marriage between Branwen and Matholwch was meant to unify two sovereign nations, but ultimately this was doomed to become a source of division and violence, instigated by the mutilation of the primary Celtic symbol of sovereignty, the horse. On a subtle and perhaps tribal consciousness level, the visceral events of the mutilation would have acted as prophecy for the forthcoming events where self-sovereignty and that of the land itself would be threatened.
- *The Cost of Betrayal:* Within the narrative Efnisien's actions appear entirely impulsive, but they act as catalyst to all forthcoming events, as the hostile enemy and chief antagoniser of the unfolding events, we may consider that Efnisien knew exactly what he was doing. And yet his actions were to ultimately lead to his undoing, but in that undoing he atoned for his brutality and died within the Cauldron of Rebirth. Within the figure of Efnisien we can see the sovereignty of the shadow, and perhaps a warning that if ignored it is likely to run amuck and cause irreparable damage to one's own sense of empowered self-sovereignty. The language of the Second Branch hints at the power and sovereignty of the shadow as a necessary compass within the self. When challenged about Efnisien's actions Brân states *'it is not easy for me either to kill or destroy him'*, implying that to do so would be to kill a necessary quality within Brân himself, the shadow.
- *The Sovereignty of Resilience and Sacrifice:* Branwen, in her calumniated state demonstrates a profound courage in the face of her suffering, her resilience is present right until the end at which point her heart breaks from sorrow. She expresses her self-sovereignty even unto death, and whilst we might consider her death as akin to 'giving up', it hides a subtle power of acceptance that

is simultaneously tragic and beautiful. Efnisien's final act of redemption highlights the complexities of human strength and frailty which are intimately tied to the notion of self-sovereignty.

- *The Tragic Cost of War and Loss:* The loss of life and the destruction of peoples and nations emphasise the futility and sorrow of conflict. War highlights the misuse of sovereignty in the othering of those perceived as the enemy, and yet paradoxically war undermines the principle of sovereignty within the instigator. The collateral damage of war upon the land further distances the people from the valued sovereignty of the land itself.

By looking at the nature of the mutilation further wisdom can be gleaned. Efnisien's cruelty in attacking the horses may appear entirely random, but it is deeply symbolic. The Second Branch is steeped in patterns of wounding and silence, and the mutilation of the horses foreshadows the future breakdown of communication, of vision and the sovereignty between Britain and Ireland. In Celtic cultures, the horse was perceived as a sacred animal, closely linked to themes of kingship and the Otherworld. They were symbols of nobility, of swiftness and the ability for humans to traverse both the physical and spiritual realms.

Efnisien's attack on the horses of Matholwch is not simply the mutilation of livestock, it is a direct targeting of sovereignty itself, this results in the undermining of the bond of marriage between Branwen and Matholwch which ultimately destabilises the sacred covenant that should have united Britain and Ireland. The precision of Efnisien's attacks is striking, he targets the head of each horse, the ears, the eyes and the lips and then turns his attention to the tails whilst leaving their bodies intact. To the ancient Celts the head was seen as the seat of the soul and the source of perception. In mutilating the heads of the horses

Efnisien is attacking perception itself, in the cutting of their tails he attacks their sense of balance, movement and their expression of life-force, these mutilations can be summarised as follows:

- *The Lips cut back to the teeth:* This symbolises the loss of coherent speech and the collapse of diplomacy and dialogue. What could have been resolved through mediation and words becomes instead a bloodbath. This is reflected in the peculiar quality that after immersion in the Cauldron of Rebirth the warriors emerge animated but dumb, the necessity of effective communication is destroyed in all cases.
- *The Ears cut down to the heads:* This is symbolic of the refusal or the inability to listen and foreshadows the failure of Britain and Ireland to hear each other's needs. Miscommunication eventually spirals into war. Efnisien as a representative of the shadow was not listened to not consulted resulting in its unruliness.
- *The eyes cut to the bone:* Without their eyelids the horses will be unable to see clearly and result in ultimate blindness. This is symbolic that neither side perceived the full consequences of their actions, and as a result both rush into destruction.
- *The tails cut to their backs:* In this act of brutality Efnisien is attacking dignity, protection and vitality. The severed tails suggest a loss of stability; things are thrown off balance from the beginning. Without their tails, the horses are exposed to pests and the elements symbolically stripping away sovereignty's protection.

All in all, we witness a desecration from head to tail, the act encompasses the animal from front to back and signals the total corruption of the sacred bond between two kingdoms. What should have been whole and dignified is now grotesque and incapable of fulfilling its true purpose. In this heinous act Efnisien symbolically strips the relationship between Britain and Ireland of its capacity to hear, see, speak and retain its balance, the four faculties required for peace. The mutilations can also be seen as an attack on communication with the indigenous Otherworld, horses were liminal creatures and often associated with the divine. By damaging their sensory organs Efnisien was severing the channels of perception between the human being and the divine. He disrupts not only political harmony but also the sacred balance between the human world and the divine realms.

Efnisien's act of violence is horribly surgical in nature, he doesn't kill the horses but rather renders them disfigured and of no use as mediators. In turn, the bond between the two kingdoms is not destroyed immediately, but rendered incoherent and broken, limping slowly but inevitably towards ultimate collapse. His focus on mutilating three parts of the horses' heads foreshadows the severing of Brân's head. As for Branwen, the mutilations symbolically echo her fate, she is silenced, beaten and humiliated in Ireland and the delicate balance between the two realms is threatened. Branwen becomes the human embodiment of the horses' wounds, she is stripped of voice, of dignity and the vision for her future.

This sequence of zoomorphic mutilation heralds the dangers of wilful miscommunication and the deliberate sabotage of relationships. In his fury Efnisien embodies the destructive forces that arise when bitterness and resentment are given free reign over sensibility. His apparent irrational attack is not against an enemy on the battlefield, but rather against the very channels of understanding and alliance. The mutilation of this primary zoomorphic symbol of sovereignty is a symbolic rupture; it is the turning point within the tale. His attack is not upon the bodies of the horses but rather their sensory capabilities, this unravels perception, communication, balance and harmony. The attack on the horses marks the beginning of a cycle of deafness, silence, blindness and unbalance that pervade the entire branch resulting in the devastation of both nations.

This sequence of events poses an interesting set of questions for the modern polytheist:

- What aspects of our lives have become blind or deaf to those who we should be in accordance with?
- How do acts of spite, bitterness and sabotage wound not only those we are in relationship with but also our own sovereignty and peace?
- What happens to us when communication is mutilated? What happens when our speech becomes incoherent and our ability to see clearly is lost?
- Inappropriate actions on our part can strip us of dignity, balance and protection, how do we reconcile our actions and reclaim our sense of self-sovereignty when they are clearly damaged?

Pigs of Plenty, Pigs of Prophecy

In addition to horses another important animal speaks subtly from the branches of the *Mabinogi,* the pig. Their appearance in the Second Branch might go wholly unnoticed, but they are present none the less and symbolise a force of influence that a reader in the 21st century may miss entirely. Within the Four Branches of the *Mabinogi* and other Welsh tales, pigs do not appear as random livestock, but indicators of the liminal, subtle clues that the reader or the listener are moving into a zone of Otherworldly influence.

Pigs punctuate the narrative of the Four Branches in a distinct and intentional manner. In the First Branch following the sequence of events that unfolds after Pwyll takes the place of the King of Annfwn, Arawn, for a year and a day, Arawn bestows upon Pwyll the title of Pwyll Pen Annwfn (Pwyll the Lord of Annwfn), who is listed in the *Triads of the Island of Britain* to possess one of the three powerful swineherds of the Island of Britain. The herd was seven strong and brought from Annwfn and gifted to Pendaran Dyfed, the adopted father of Pwyll and Rhiannon's son Pryderi.[13] The implication here is that the pigs were a gift from the Otherworld and that pigs are not an indigenous species of our planet. In the Third Branch it is the appearance of a splendid white boar that leads Pryderi and Manawydan to a magical fort in which Pryderi and eventually Rhiannon become captives. In the Fourth Branch, the stealing of pigs from the south instigates a war between the kingdoms of north and south Wales. Later, Gwydion follows a great white sow to the feet of the World Tree to rescue his fostered child, Lleu Llaw Gyffes. In each case, the appearance of pigs indicate that all is not as it seems, as creatures of Otherworldly origin, their presence is a subtle but potent indicator of the thinning of veils between worlds.

In the Second Branch a whole host of zoomorphic influences are present to guide the listener into the thin places between worlds. Their appearance in the tale of Branwen is so subtle that they are easily overlooked as a minor or insignificant detail. The lines that follow from the text of the *Mabinogi* punctuate the story with a small but vital detail:

> *A meicheit Matholwch a oedynt ar lan y weilgi dydgueith, yn troi yg kylch eu moch. Ac o achaws e dremynt a welsant ar y weilgi, wy a doethant at Matholwch.*[14]
> Matholwch's swineherds were on the seashore one day, busy with their pigs. And because of what they saw on the sea, they went to Matholwch.

The discerning reader will note that once again the term for sea in the original text is the mutation for gweilgi, carrying as it does the implication that we are not in fact dealing with merely the body of water that separates Britain from Ireland. To a medieval audience another clue would have been obvious within the narrative. It would seem incongruous that the swineherds would have been driven onto the bare sands and mudflats of the Irish coast, surely fishermen would have been a more plausible narrative. But it is precisely this incongruity that heralds a shift in perspective. To witness or be told of swine appearing where they evidently do not belong is a clue that reminds the listener that the scene has undergone a significant shift, ordinary rules no longer apply from the moment of their appearance. In the Second Branch, various zoomorphic influences punctuate the narrative, but to a medieval audience it would be the pig that carried the most weight of influence.

Matholwch's swineherds provide the narrative with a reminder that we are no longer dealing with the realm of humans, but rather with the realm of gods and mysteries. They carry an unmistakable scent of the Otherworld. Not only do they stand as symbols of human sustenance, but they also concurrently embody sovereignty that is transferred across worlds. We can deduce that the storyteller's choice of swineherds as opposed to fishermen, shell-gatherers or kelp farmers is quite deliberate, it acts as a storytelling device that reminds the audience that they are standing at the threshold of a mythic reality, rooted in the Otherworld. The pigs act as creatures of transition, they herald a disruption to the natural order of the apparent world and act as agents of Otherworldly sovereignty.

In addition, this questions the reality or nature of the physical locations which are used simply as narrative devices. A quick search through history will reveal that there never was a war between Britain and Ireland to an extent that Ireland was decimated to only five surviving pregnant women and obliterated the British armies. Ireland is positioned within the narrative as the proxy otherworld, located from the perspective of the British across the seas to the west, the direction and location of the Otherworld in several Celtic cultural myth and folklore. Ireland is positioned as a narrative device, what is being alluded to by the themes above is that we are not dealing with the physical island of Ireland but rather witnessing a journey to the Otherworld, or at least one of the islands contained within it.

This requires an additional note to expand and deepen this concept. Within the collection of medieval Welsh poetry attributed to the legendary poet Taliesin, *Llyfr Taliesin* (The Book of Taliesin)[15] we encounter a journey to the Otherworld in search of the elusive great cauldron of mystery, magic and transformation. The poem is titled *Preiddeu Annwfn* (The Spoils of Annwfn), and whilst they are often treated as distinct and somewhat separate works, one belonging to the cyfarwydd (storytelling) tradition and the other firmly rooted in the Welsh Bardic Tradition. One is presented as prose the other as a cryptic poem in strict metre. However, when read in comparison it is apparent that the Second Branch in many ways acts as the 'movie version' of the *Spoils of Annwfn,* which concerns a journey across the sea to several Otherworldly islands, the confrontation with hostile forces and the search for a cauldron in the guardianship of nine mystical maidens who warm and kindle the cauldron by their breath. The great Cauldron[16] of the Otherworld is a common motif in Celtic mythology and folklore, but it does not act as merely a vessel for culinary purposes, and neither is it wholly a symbol of magic. Instead, it acts as an axis of sovereignty, transformation and survival. Whosoever controls the great Cauldron controls life itself. To lose or be unable to find the Cauldron is to forfeit sovereignty; to find and retain it is to possess the very keys to destiny. This journey is perilous and in both the Second Branch and the *Spoils of Annwfn* only seven individuals survive the journey and return to Britain.

The Stupefaction of Sovereignty

A term that is commonly used in any exploration of applicable myth is sovereignty, but this may bewilder rather than illuminate. Whilst this discourse has made frequent reference to the term it is important that we unpackage it at this juncture to make sense of its meaning and significance within our journey with myth.

The concept of sovereignty can be broken down into four distinct but interwoven qualities:

1. *The Cauldron* – The Cauldron is not simply a magical object but rather the primary symbol for the presence of the Otherworld within us. It represents the life-force, the great mysteries of death, rebirth and transformation. It is the primary vessel for the Welsh force of divine inspiration, Awen, which is claimed to have its origin in the Otherworld. The cauldron does not refer to external kingship but rather to the inner capacity to be our whole and authentic selves. When we tend the Cauldron, we are tending the soul itself. Thus, the Caudron is the primary axis of sovereignty that is simultaneously intrinsic and extrinsic.
2. *Zoomorphic Representations* – Animals act as portents or mirrors of sovereignty, they appear as threshold moments announcing the presence of the Otherworld, they are harbingers of mystery. At times they may act as a warning that Otherworldly forces are imminently arriving, they punctuate the mundane world as clear signals that one must stop and pay attention. Different animals will carry the weight of different meaning. Pigs mark an intrusion of the Otherworld, horses are bound with the status of sovereignty, and birds act as liminal carriers between two worlds.

3. *Voyages and Thresholds* – Sovereignty is never static but in a constant state of flux and transition. Sea-crossings and liminal settings such as the rock of Harlech are contexts in which sovereignty is put to the test. The voyages are often perilous, plunging one into the abyss where every aspect of the traveller is brought into question. They imply that for sovereignty to be maintained and preserved one must undergo a voyage that requires courage and bravery.
4. *Anthropomorphic Representations* – Human-like figures bring a relational quality to the tales, within the human appearing figures we can see mirrors of ourselves. Brân can be seen as the masculine and active concept of self-sovereignty; Branwen is its feminine and receptive nature. One directs whilst the other receives. A third principles exists and can be seen embodied within figures like Manawydan, Nisien and Efnisien, they present the ethereal or energetic quality between the apparent binary forces of Brân and Branwen. This creates a tertiary force that moves beyond the binary. These are the messengers of self-sovereignty and our ability to live full and empowered lives that are guided by one's virtues, dignity and inner truth, it expresses authorship over oneself. This concept lies at the heart of the myths. The Cauldron, the animals and voyages of the spirit and soul are used as symbolic languages that direct us to truth. They remind us that our task within this life is not to control that which is fated for us, but rather to remain whole within ourselves as we meet it.

As we consider the above, we can bring the hidden meaning and symbolism of these concepts into the lived reality of the polytheist by contemplating the following:

- What animals, real or symbolic have appeared in your own life as signs or mirrors of change?

- How do you recognise that when something in your life is acting as a warning that your self-sovereignty is being threatened or addressed?
- Identity the periods in your life that felt like a crossing or a threshold into the unknown.
- How did you respond to these 'voyages? Did you carry your dignity and resilience with you, or did you feel that they were threatened or questioned?
- Which aspects of your life feel most aligned with your true and authentic self?
- Are there aspects of your life that feel diminished or as if you were living a half-truth? What might be required of you to reclaim those parts of yourself?
- With the Cauldron representing the soul itself, what 'fire' in your life tends and warms it?
- How might embracing your self-sovereignty allow you to move through challenges, sorrow and grief differently?

Following on from our discourse of Otherworldly and Zoomorphic influences on the tale of Branwen, we now take flight into the mysteries and wisdom of corvids, which will deepen our understanding of the themes of sovereignty that course through this tale.

Chapter 6

Of Severed Heads and Corvids

Contrary to what one might expect, our next voyage in our journey with Branwen and her family is neither to Ireland or the mountains and islands of northwest Wales, but rather, we venture to the current capital city of the United Kingdom, London. It is here that we can see tendrils of myth woven into the fabric of secular British society and deepen our understanding of the power of myth to persist.

In the heart of the city of London, mere yards away from the bustle of shops, theatres and tourist attractions, sits the ominous and majestic Tower of London. Adjacent to the river Thames, it stands as a symbol of authority, justice and guardianship and since 1661 has been the home of the crown jewels of the British monarchy. But a distant mythic cry can still be heard from its turrets as ravens continue to call from its battlements. Today, and traditionally, seven ravens freely roam the Tower of London, they are fed, cared for and watched over by the raven master of the Yeoman Warders. I draw your attention to the number of ravens required to maintain their apotropaic role, seven, a number that oddly emulates the number of survivors in Brân's retinue and the seven survivors mentioned in the poem *Preiddeu Annwfn*. Legend says that if the ravens were ever to depart the Tower it would herald the fall of Britain. It adds a magical element to any visit to the Tower; a quaint tradition steeped in folklore and tourist theatre. But beneath the veneer of tourists and snapping cameras hides an older truth for these ravens are an echo of a deeper mystery, one that reaches back to the Second Branch of the *Mabinogi* and the *Children of Llŷr*.

At the heart of this mystery lies the echo of Brân the Blessed, the Raven King, whose gigantic body bridges the waters between this world and the other, and whose severed head was said to be buried within the White Mount, today's Tower Hill, and therein to protect these islands forever. His sister Branwen is not omitted from this mystery, for in her sorrow and profound sacrifice we see a mirroring of Brân, her story is also tied to the fate of Britain as both a physical location and a metaphor.

The ravens of the Tower of London whisper of a deeper and darker secret, one intimately connected to the myth of Brân, it was at or near the Tower that those condemned by the crown were beheaded. This gruesome act of corporal punishment echoes with the memory of Brân's head buried beneath its blood-stained soil. The Celts regarded the head as the seat of the soul, the vessel of wisdom and power. Warriors took the heads of their enemies as trophies not out of cruelty, but as acts of spiritual possession. To own the head was to hold the essence. In Brân, this belief reaches its mythic extreme, for even in death his head retains life, wisdom, and guardianship as it continues to counsel his retinue on the magical island of Gwales.

The Severed Head and the White Mount.

At the conclusion of the battle in Ireland and the fateful blow dealt to Brân the cyfarwydd tells us:

> *Then Bendigeidfran ordered that his head be cut off. 'Take my head' he said, 'and carry it to the Gwynfryn (White hill) in London and bury it with its face towards France.*[17]

After decades of counsel the head dies when the doors towards Cornwall are opened, his retinue carry the head to London to fulfil his wishes. However, this is no ordinary internment, this is an act of apotropaic magic, the head serves as a magical talisman defending the island of Britain from foreign invasion. Simultaneously the head transforms into a powerful symbol of the oral, storytelling and Bardic traditions, an entity that is both dead and alive, alive but also dead. The symbolism is profound on many levels and elements of it are maintained in modernity. The Tower of London stands at the heart of the British nation, and yet beneath its foundations lies the memory of Brân.

The Second Branch continues:

> *And that was one of the Three Fortunate Concealments when it was concealed, and one of the Three Unfortunate Disclosures when it was disclosed, for no oppression would ever come across the sea to this island while the head was in that hiding place.*[18]

This is expanded upon in the earlier collection *The Triads of the Island of Britain* which says:

> *The Three Fortunate Concealments of the Island of Britain:*
> *The Head of Bendigedfran, son of Llŷr, which was concealed in the White Hill in London with its face towards France. And as long as it was in the position in which it was put there, not oppression would every come to this island.*
> *And one of the Three Unfortunate Disclosures when Arthur disclosed the Head of Bendigeidfran from the White Hill, because it did not seem right to him that his island, should be defended by the strength of anyone, but by his own.*[19]

In learning of Brân's protective power, Arthus chooses to unearth it, but to remove Brân's head acted as a symbolic severing of Britain's ancestral guardianship. Perhaps Arthur symbolises a shift in culture where the sense of the divine was changing with the rise of Christianity. It may be indicative of a socio-political change from collective sovereignty rooted in the old gods and the ancestors to personal sovereignty embodied in a single and heroic king. Arthur's pride ruptures the old order and severs the protection once afforded by the Raven King. Britain is left magically and physically vulnerable and is subsequently invaded repeatedly. The element of the myth may be a remnant of an older form of apotropaic magic or may be reflecting a narrative of crisis and challenges that the British faced, pointing a finger of blame at the legendary Arthur.

Arthur's disclosure of Brân's head raises some troubling questions:

- What happens when ancestral covenants are irreparably broken?
- What is it that becomes lost when human ambition supplants that of divine guardianship?
- What reparations, if any, can be conducted to reclaim order to that which is broken?
- Can sovereignty every truly to confined to the self, or is it intimately tied to the gods, the ancestors and the land itself?
- What do we lose when we unearth, dismiss and discard symbols of ancestral guardianship?

It is easy, or perhaps foolhardy to consider that these are merely tales, conflated by time, hidden agendas and centuries of retelling, and yet the power of myth to persist is evident. In modernity, Britian continues to tend to the myths contained in the Second Branch, however unconsciously. Brân may have been betrayed by Arthur and his unfortunate disclosure, but his birds remain, their cries whispering of an older magic intimately tied to the land of Britain and its seat of power. Their presence and protection continue to tie modern day London to the mysteries of the Second Branch.

In this way, Britain still tends the myth, however unconsciously. The Raven King may have been betrayed, but his symbolic birds bind modern London to the mysteries of the Second Branch. For the modern polytheist these ancient stories express profound guidance. The severed head of Brân teaches us that protection is rooted in sacrifice and that guardianship comes at a cost. Branwen's sorrow reveals that suffering can also give rise to healing when integrated with integrity and sincerity into the very fabric of life. Although Branwen is long dead by the time Brân's head is buried in London, the two events are intimately connected, they are threads woven into the same cloth. Branwen's silence is mirrored in her brother's supernatural voice, her mystery of death mirrored in his undying. Whilst seemingly absent from the concluding section of the narrative, she persists into modern times symbolically and in spirit through the figure of the Corvus. Death does not separate the siblings; they are two halves of the same coin. Together they reveal that sovereignty is not restricted or limited to the power of rule by monarchs, but hint at a persistence of kinship, of sacrifice and sorrow that guards a people through the corridors of time.

It is in the Corvid mysteries, where modern mythic practises echo with the songs of the old world, that the inseparable nature of Brân and Branwen finds its deepest meaning. The Corvus does not refer to one bird alone, but instead to an entire family, not to a single figure but to a lineage, the corvid family of the Second Branch and their mysterious songs continue to shape Britain's mythic heart to this day.

The Cry of the Corvids

To deepen our understanding of Branwen we must also consider not only the role of her brother, but also the hidden meanings of their names. Welsh words convey significantly more than mere nouns or adjectives; they are multilayered, and, in their examination, we can glean a wisdom that may have initially eluded us.

Brân and Branwen appear in several manuscripts during the medieval period, spanning the storytelling and Bardic tradition respectively. Their presence in both schools suggests that they were commonly known and understood within Welsh culture from a folkloric and storytelling perspective and within the disciplined practises and structure of Welsh Bardism.

The Second Branch of the *Mabinogi* opens by directly naming Brân:

> *Bendigeidfran fab Llŷr, a oedd frenin coronawc ar yr ynys hon, ac ardyrchawc o goron Lundein.*[20]
> Bendigeidfran the son of Llŷr, was the crowned kind over this island, and invested with the crown of London.[21]

The name Bendigeidfran is derived from two words – *bendigeid* (bendigaid in modern Welsh) meaning something that is worthy of worship or praise, glorious, blessed, beatified, sacred or holy. It carries a secondary meaning that is frequently used in the description of healing plants. Whilst it is not explicitly attested that Brân has healing qualities, the sequence of events on the magical island of Gwales could be perceived as a process of healing the seven survivors with the head of Brân sitting centre stage.

Bendigeid is followed by the term *bran*[22] which refers to members of the *Corvus* family of birds. In Welsh Brân might refer to any of the eight species of common corvids in the United Kingdom, which are:

- Carrion crows
- Rooks
- Jackdaws
- Magpies

- Ravens
- Jays
- Hooded crows
- Coughs[23]

Grammatically the term Bendigeidfran would be rendered as 'the blessed or holy corvid' in English, and whilst his name appears in various forms, Brân Bendigeid, Brân fab Llŷr; within the *White Book of Rhydderch* and in the *Triads of the Islands of Britain* it appears consistently as Bendigeidfran, with Brân son of Llŷr being the preferred choice of the poets and the current author of this work. Within the vernacular of Welsh culture, he is more commonly referred to as capitalised Brân, which can be seen consistently throughout this book.

Rachel Bromwich suggests that bendigeid might be a corruption of *pen* (head) with a following epithet, owing to the symbolic significance of Brân's head as a blessed talisman.[24] Other hypothesis has suggested that bendigeid refers to the later meaning that Brân was responsible for the introduction of Christianity to the British Isles, although this claim cannot be attested to a time prior to the 18th Century. Whilst the evolution of his name might echo with whispers from ancient times conflated with the medieval and early modern period, it is generally accepted that the figure of Brân is a euhemerized deity.[25] In common Welsh and British lore, Brân is often imagined as a raven, and whilst this is not explicit within the myths or poetry, it is taken for granted. This may be in part due to the raven being the largest species of Corvus in the British Isles, the giant amongst that group of birds, emulates the quality of the mythic Brân. In addition, the raven in common Celtic myth and folklore is a bird associated with battle, prophecy and of sovereignty, a liminal and perhaps psychopompic quality perched between the threshold of life and death. In this manner it is a fitting symbolic comparison where Brân embodies the raven's role as a guardian of the Islands of the Mighty and a keeper of sovereignty.

However, if Brân is emblematic of the raven, then what of his sister Branwen? Her name contains the prefix 'bran', which we have already attested to mean any member of the Corvus family. Whereas the suffix 'wen' expresses a quality that is blessed or holy reflecting the attributes bestowed on her brother by means of bendigeid. However, it is unclear what the original designation of her name was in antiquity, one instance of her name as 'Bronwen' meaning 'white breast' appears in the *White Book of Rhydderch,* and whilst some scholars have speculated that this may well have been the original form of her name, and the later Branwen was influenced by proxy of her brother, she is consistently referred to as Branwen in both the storytelling and Bardic traditions. Scholarly speculations have suggested that the form Branwen is apparently old and that Bendigeidfran may be post-Christian. Other arguments have hypothesised that Brân and Branwen may have evolved from a singular native element subjected to linguistic and social evolution and development.[26] Whatever the origin, for the modern polytheist we can justifiably connect with both elements as interconnected deities of modernity with echoes of ancestral origin. With the general scholarly consensus being that her name is accepted as Branwen, meaning blessed or holy Corvus, we might ponder which member of the corvid family best reflects her story and attributes. It may be tempting to consider that she is also associated with the raven, but from my own unverified personal gnosis I believe that a deeper wisdom can be gleaned by considering a different association. This book has demonstrated thus far that we can learn much from the animals that appear in the myths, and in doing so we move into relationship with those creatures who share this planet with us. When considering Branwen in relationality with corvids, it is the smaller and often overlooked jackdaw that I turn to your attention.

The jackdaw is the smallest of the Corvus family, with a distinctive silvery sheen to the back of its head, slight with startlingly bright grey eyes, they are renowned for their playful chatter, their intelligence and deep bonds of loyalty. Jackdaws tend to pair for life and live in constant companionship. They are less nervous of humans than the other Corvus members, and tend to make their homes in liminal places, chimneys, towers, ruins etc. They often live close to human populations whilst embodying a subtle liminality. This quality reflects Branwen beautifully, as she too inhabits the betwixt and between, flitting between sovereignty and subjugation, between her divine heritage and that of mortal suffering.

When we consider her story, it is not one of Braun or brute force, but rather of endurance and loyalty, she possesses a natural gift of communication, particularly with the realm of birds. This is exemplified in her training a starling to carry a message to her brother. In Welsh the starling is called the *drudwen,* meaning the blessed or holy druid, a bird that is intimately connected to the wisdom traditions of ancient Britain, held in the guise of the oak-wise Druid. Akin to the jackdaw, the starling is a small bird, one with a distinct call and renowned for their mysterious murmuration, where they can gather in flocks of tens of thousands of individuals that form great clouds of movement.

Together, Brân as the Raven King is vast, prophetic, a figure of active sovereignty, counsel, a figure that accepts his fate and uses his own incurable wound to soothe and heal others. Branwen is the blessed, holy jackdaw, slight but loyal, communicative and compassionate, she represents receptive sovereignty whilst embodying both sorrow and the profundity of symbiotic relationships. While one towers, the other endures. Brân embodies the might of kingship and the acceptance of fate, and Branwen expresses the virtues and resilience of the often overlooked. Neither one exists in a vacuum, their union reveals the whole of sovereignty, on one hand we see the grandeur of rule and the sacredness of sacrifice, on the other we witness the quieter but harder truth where sovereignty survives sorrow with dignity.

To summarise this chapter, masculine self-sovereignty as embodied in Brân, expresses the capacity that one has to uphold and protect the integrity of one's own authentic being. It is the ability to direct one's actions assertively with gentle power as opposed to sheer Braun. Feminine self-sovereignty is reflected through the figure of Branwen and expresses the art of maintaining the whole of ones being amid fragmentation. She emulates our ability to maintain dignity and presence even when all around us appears wounded and unstable. However, swimming between these two poles are the forces of Efnisien and Nisien, the twins of shadow and light, these are the unpredictable and stable forces of the human psyche held in precarious balance.

They express the destructive and harmonious forces within each of us. Within these figures we discover the inner tests that sovereignty demands. True sovereignty is neither masculine nor feminine but is rather the dynamic balance of both forces which are counter-balanced and mediated by the influence of Efnisien/Nisien. As a tertiary force they teach us that we each hold the capacity for creation and destruction, for compassion and indifference. When all three forces are reconciled within the self, we become an island of our own might, a sacred vessel upon the sea of existence.

Chapter 7

The Bird with Clipped Wings

Calumniation and Accusation in the Second Branch

In this chapter we move into the exploration of the most difficult aspects of the Second Branch and a common theme that streams through the *Mabinogi*, that of calumniation and accusation. In dissecting these problematic themes, we consider the question, what does it mean when women in myth carry the burden of blame and irrational accusation, even when said women act with dignity?

In the Second Branch we follow the story of Branwen whose sovereignty is stripped from her, her voice is silenced, and her dignity is broken to the extent that her heart eventually breaks. However, she is not alone in this fate, for in the First Branch we are introduced to Rhiannon who also endured humiliation and slander, a figure who is falsely accused of murdering and devouring her own child and consequently condemned to serve as a beast of burden, carrying all newcomers to the court on her back and retelling her story of shame, reinforcing her humiliation. Her story mirrors that of Branwen, and vice-versa. Both women stand as parallel witnesses and victims to the theme of calumniation.

Calumniation is the act of making false and malicious statements against another person for the sole purpose of destroying their reputation and good standing. In the First and Second Branch, though their stories follow a different trajectory, Branwen and Rhiannon suffer a similar ordeal, both are women of dignity and sovereignty who are reduced through their humiliation and forced to carry the weight of blame for the dysfunction of others. When looked at side by side, we can see that the *Mabinogi* and other myths are not simply recounting tragedies that occur in isolation, but instead, they hold up a mirror to a recurring pattern of human behaviour. What we witness in the pages of myth continue to be true today, where families, societies and individuals place blame on someone else, rather than face the weight of their own shadows and shortcomings.

At times, myths can feel remote, reaching through the mists of time where customs and practices seem unapplicable to a modern audience, yet their tenacity to portray elements of the human condition are truly timeless. When we look closer at myth, we can perceive that the same pattern of idiosyncrasies and motivations apply today as they did a thousand years ago. We may believe we are distant from these ancestral tales, and yet we live in an age where reputations can be destroyed in mere seconds by a click of a computer or a comment on a social media page.

The power of the internet can shape narratives, often by the loudest voices, not by truth, but for the sole purpose of 'cancelling' another individual. Modern 'cancel culture' echoes with the same sense of social shaming that emulate the mechanisms of calumniation. Human beings have consistently been driven to cast blame upon another, to cause another individual to be othered or scapegoated into submission. When a person relieves their fear or anger by isolating another person as the bearer of shame, the personal and collective collateral damage can be devastating. This narrative affirms the position of the perpetrator and affirms their stance as the one who holds the most power, and yet this power is unfounded and arising from a place of insecurity rather than authenticity.

To be calumniated is to be stripped of one's sovereignty, in Branwen's case, she is subjected to beatings that silence her, she is forced to live as a servant where her social status is stripped from her. When we look at Rhiannon, we can see a similar theme where she is also stripped of her status and forced into a submission that reinforces her imposed shame and embarrassment. In both cases we witness the horrors that happen when an individual or group of people feel the need to blame and scapegoat another, attacking their sovereignty and stripping them of their reputation, it reflects a deep and unsettling inability to face responsibilities or deal with unresolved tensions. The myths act as a stark warning expressing how the cost of calumniation can break communities and lead to the horror of war where the sovereignty of all parties is ultimately reduced and broken. When perceived from this angle, Branwen's story is not reflecting the tale of an ancient figure, it is a story about us. When we move into the wisdom of myth it asks us to ponder:

- When and why do we believe false narratives about others?
- Why do we participate in the silencing and shaming of another's sovereignty?

These questions and the lessons that arise from them are as urgent now as they were in medieval Wales. The implication is that sovereignty, whether personal or collective is a fragile thing. It must be guarded, not only for the sake of ourselves but also for each other. When we deny the sovereignty of another, we run the risk of denying and damaging our own.

This carries a deeper and immanent truth, within the *Mabinogi*, Branwen and Rhiannon are not guilty, they have done nothing to deserve their heinous calumniation. And yet, guilt is irrelevant when a group or individual with an agenda is looking for someone to carry the weight of their own misgivings. In the scapegoating of these two women in the *Mabinogi* as representatives of the sovereign feminine, the perpetrator attains a sense of restoration to that which they deem is broken, but this temporary fix will ultimately fail for it rests on falsehood. The parallels between Branwen and Rhiannon are particularly striking for both women enter marriages that carry significant political weight. Two women who were revered as beautiful and noble have their sovereignty stripped from them, they are dehumanised by the agendas and failures of the men that surround them.

From a mythic perspective what we are witnessing is the othering of sovereignty itself. The Queen is made a servant, the divine is diminished and denigrated as other. Beneath these acts of calumniation hides a darker shadow and truth, for in their degradation lies a flaw of the human condition; when sovereignty is misunderstood it becomes something to fear, to diminish or enslave. When we read of the fate of Branwen and Rhiannon, we can glean that their worth is measured only by how they serve the needs of others. As representatives of the feminine principle of sovereignty their calumniation arises when said principle is unacknowledged leading to its distortion and degradation. Whilst their sovereignty is not destroyed, it is nonetheless pushed to the margins and no longer heard in the great halls but forced instead to whisper its mysteries from the shadows. When sovereignty is denied, it transforms into an expression of sorrow, and in that sorrowness the land itself consequently suffers. In the tale of Branwen this sorrow spreads across two nations consuming both Britian and Ireland in a dreadful war. When we turn our attention to Rhiannon, we see that the land itself is left without its rightful heir until her truth wins out.

The othering of sovereignty speaks to us as modern polytheists and raises significant questions:

- How often do we exile the parts of ourselves that represent our inner sovereignty?

- How often have you experienced a denigration of your intuition and dignity because they may be perceived as inconvenient or misunderstood?
- In your experience how often have you encountered personally or indirectly the silencing of women's voices?

The message that arises from the calumniation of Branwen and Rhiannon reminds us that sovereignty cannot be wholly erased, it can be supressed, it can be punished and ridiculed, but throughout any denigration its presence remains. In these stories we see the cost of denying sovereignty, not only for the individual who suffers calumniation but for the entire community that refuses to honour or acknowledge it. The denigration of sovereignty leads inevitably to collateral damage that seeps into the very fabric of the individuals or group that instigated it.

Branwen's sovereignty expresses the right to live with dignity and wholeness; her story reminds us of what can happen when that sovereignty is denied and denigrated. When we consider this from an immanent perspective we may glean some useful wisdom, whilst calumniation can arise from an extrinsic course i.e. placed upon us by others, it can also be intrinsic where we calumniate ourselves and deny our own sense of self-sovereignty. In modern life this can be seen as an addiction to anxiety, where anxiety and anxiousness can become identifying aspects of our personality. The inner saboteur who shouts incessantly to remind us of our flaws. The assertion of narratives that affirm our identity as victim. When left unchecked and undealt with these can chronically lead to burnout and depression and a continuous denial of our own self-sovereignty. The result of this denial impacts not only the individual but can often ripple out collaterally to affect families, communities and societies.

When we consider the feminine principle of self-sovereignty it is also important to rise above the notion of strict gender roles.

All expressions of gender contain the active/masculine, and receptive/feminine qualities of self-sovereignty, and swimming between them is the third principle embodied by Efnisien and Nisien. With this in mind, feminine sovereignty is not limited to women's issues alone, although in the making of that statement it is important to consider that women have borne the brunt of diminishment and calumniation through history. From a spiritual perspective the feminine principle of sovereignty is that part of us that knows our inherent worth, it is the claiming and re-claiming of our own unique voice. It is the part of us that insists on the dignity of our inner, authentic self. When we stand in our sovereignty, we refuse to exile our intuition, we value the quality of grief as a genuine response to loss, we acknowledge our capacity to sustain, nourish and nurture ourselves and others. These are not inferior to the masculine principle of sovereignty but are requirements for that principle to be expressed honourably and with integrity. They are two sides of the same coin. When we live with awareness of feminine sovereignty, we are more likely to listen to the voices around us that have been silenced, to make reparations where dignity has been stripped away.

In the tales we see this element denied primarily to women, and when we deny it in women, we also deny it in humanity itself. Branwen and her mythic sister Rhiannon stand not only as powerful warnings but also as guides to traverse the double-edged sword of sovereignty. When perceived as a whole, the women of the *Mabinogi* stand not only as warnings but also as guides. Through their stories we can see that whilst sovereignty can be diminished it does not die entirely. Instead, it waits for recognition and waits for us to reclaim it. It is only when we reclaim our sovereignty that we move towards restoring balance within ourselves, and in doing that we begin to heal the wider world around us, for ultimately the sovereignty of the self is bound with the sovereignty of all.

In making the above applicable and relevant to the modern polytheist, we must move into an awareness of feminine sovereignty and listen to those voices around us that have been silenced. When we give dignity where it has been stripped, we honour the inner queen or goddess that resides within ourselves and others. In doing so we stand in the power of our sovereignty and refuse to exile out intuition, our grief and our capacity to nurture and nourish. Whilst these traits may for some be perceived as weaknesses, they are anything but, rather, they express the very strengths that maintain our humanity.

Bridging the Myth and the Self

Within the story of Branwen, and of Rhiannon who mirrors her, we are not merely witnessing an old sorrow that has been preserved in the embers of time, but rather we are being invited to experience a living truth. As Branwen's songs rises from the pages of myth into immanency, we can shift our perspective to experience her calumniation within the mythic landscape of the self. Both Branwen and Rhiannon carry the memory of what it means to lose one's voice, to have ones' dignity stripped away, to have one's rightful place in the world diminished and denigrated, and yet through all of this, we can sense a quiet resilience and sense of endurance. Branwen reminds us that sovereignty is not a crown that is bestowed from without, but an inner flame that must be tended.

The following ritual acts as a bridge between the myth and one's lived experience, bringing the wisdom of the myth into the present moment. This is the power of applied myth, when we consciously move into their currents which continue to pass through time like a silver thread. When we step into the perpetual flow of myth we can recognise the moments in our lives where we too have been calumniated and diminished, when our voices have been silenced, and in doing so we may remember the sacred fires of sovereignty that still burn beneath the ashes of calumniation.

This ritual is not about worship, but about remembrance, it is not an act of invoking ancient gods, but rather of awakening to the part of us that knows dignity, compassion and truth. By using simple symbols, flame, water and stone, we call that inner knowing and whisper as Branwen once did upon the shores of sorrow – *"Though I have been broken, I remain whole and retain my sovereignty."* It can be used to reclaim your sovereignty when you feel that it has been diminished or affected by circumstances around or within you.

Ritual for Reclaiming Sovereignty

For the following ritual you will need:

- A white candle to represent sovereignty and dignity.
- A small bowl or cauldron of water to represent Branwen's tears and for the sea that connects us to her and the power of myth.
- A small stone or pebble to represent the grounded self.

Instructions:

1. Prepare your space in a manner by which you are accustomed, ensuring you will not be disturbed. Once your space has been prepared sit quietly within it and position the candle directly in front of you, the bowl or cauldron to its left and the stone to the right. Take three deep breaths, one with the land beneath, a second with the sky above you and a third with the seas that surround you. Allow your body to settle into the moment and into the space you have prepared.
2. Bring to mind an image of Branwen, allow the image to appear of its own volition. This is how Branwen appears

to you. As you focus on the image say the following or similar words – *"I call to you Branwen, sister of sorrows, healer of souls, arise and come unto me, bestow upon me your wisdom and your sovereignty."* Breathe deeply and repeat the above as often as you feel is necessary.

3. Take another deep breath and light the candle, position your hands either side of the flame in a cupping gesture feeling the heat from the flame and say – *"I call upon the light of sovereignty within me, though it may be diminished, it cannot and will not be destroyed."* Take two more deep breaths, repeating the above as many as times as you feel necessary.
4. Position your hands in a cupping gesture around the bowl or cauldron, breathing deeply as you do. Dip the index and middle fingers of your right hand into the water and let a few drops fall onto the stone or pebble. As you do repeat the following or similar words – *"Like Branwen, I too have known sorrow, and I have known diminishment. Yet, I endure, and I remain whole."* Breathe deeply, becoming aware of the power of breath within you and the resonance of the words. Repeat the affirmation as many times as you feel necessary.
5. Take the stone or pebble into your right hand and position your left hand over it. Breathe deeply as you fell its weight and texture and its steadiness. Imagine that it glows with an inner light to represent the power of your sovereignty. Say the following or similar – *"This is my sovereignty, I will not abandon it, I shall carry it within me, I shall stand in its power."* Continue to breathe deeply and consciously repeating the phrase as often as you feel necessary.
6. Place the stone back in its original position and remain in the space for several minutes. As you do, consider that the three objects before you represent the three parts of yourself, your inner light, your emotional landscape and

how you are grounded in your own sovereignty. Take a moment to feel them unite.

7. To close the ritual, offer Branwen your thanks in your own words, extinguish the candle, keep the stone as a reminder of your dignity and sovereignty and when time permits pour the water onto the land.

Despite her calumniation and diminishment there is a message of resilience and endurance that arises from her tale. Within the Second Branch of the *Mabinogi,* we are introduced to Branwen as one of the Three Chief Ancestors of the Island of Britain, a theme that will be explored more fully later. Her sovereignty does not lie in the avoidance of sorrow, but in enduring it with dignity. Whilst she embodies the broken vessel of sovereignty, so too will her son Gwern, carry this fragile covenant, only to be brutally cast into the fire, a shocking act that conceals a deeper mystery that we must now turn our attention to.

Chapter 8

Gwern – The Alder Child

Perhaps the most haunting moment in the Second Branch is the cruel and shocking death of Branwen's only child – Gwern. Not only are we witness to the burning of any bridges of reconciliation between Britain and Ireland that his birth marked, but also any promise of renewal. A palpable tension increases as the shadow brother, Efnisien, and his spider-senses anticipates an ulterior motive within the gigantic house of a hundred columns, built to accommodate the massive form of Brân. After enduring humiliation and exile, the birth of Gwern should have acted as the union of two nations, but this fragile hope is shattered when Efnisien throws the young boy into the fire at the centre of the great house, what ensues is devastating carnage and unmitigated collateral damage.

As modern readers it is almost impossible to reconcile the unbearable violence with any symbolic meanings, and yet, significant meaning can be found swimming within this horrific scene. From a mythic perspective fire is not simple destruction but rather a transformative device, what we are witnessing here is something being burned away, but what exactly might that be? To discover the meaning of this devastating scene and be placed in accordance with its wisdom we must dissect the details of this scene down to their constituent parts. In doing so we also pass through the flames of the House of the Hundred Columns and allow the fire to reveal the deeper meaning that is secreted within its scorching heat.

Can meaning be found in the murder of a young child? If we turn to the work of Will Parker in his exploration of the Four Branches of the *Mabinogi,* he suggests that the entire scene has an irrational quality to it, implying that it contains a deeper and magical significance, he goes on to elaborate that the destruction of Gwern may be indicative of a *'dimly-visible pre Christian tradition of possible Druidic provenance.'*[27] Therefore, in order for us to discover the wisdom of this scene we must delve into meaning of the name of Branwen's son, Gwern, and its mystical associations within the Welsh Bardic and storytelling traditions.

The Child of Alder

The child's name literally means alder; it is within his name that mystery is revealed. Alder is a tree of water and of blood, it represents concealment, protection and revelation. The alder grows along the borders of rivers and thrives in swampy ground and marshlands. As a tree that stands at the threshold where one realm dissolves into another it expresses a liminal quality, a tree that is betwixt and between. For the Celts, the alder was a vital resource providing wood that does not rot in water but rather becomes as hard as stone. The entire foundations of the city of Venice consists of alder pillars that have hardened over centuries to support the city. Where other woods would rot quickly, alder serves as a foundation to buildings and bridges providing it with a liminal quality.

As a liminal symbol, a being neither of the land nor of water, it acts as a bridge between both realms. In Irish myth, Deirdre of the Sorrows fled with Naoise to the alder woods of Glen Etibhe in Alba (Scotland), to seek refuge and sanctuary from the wrath of King Conchobhar. In Irish Gaelic the term for alder if *fearn* which bears a striking similarity to the sound of Gwern in Welsh. Alder groves were simultaneously respected and feared as liminal and magical places, making them the perfect ground for the outcast and the scapegoated to seek solace and safety.

In addition, the leaves and cones of alder can be utilised as a dye, with the cones yielding a deep caramel colour and the leaves a pale green dye. Effective for dying garments which in turn provided natural camouflage, the alder was a vital resource not only in colouring clothing but as a strategic device in rendering the garments invisible to hostile eyes in woodland settings. For the modern animist, the qualities of alder can be perceived as having both literal and magical camouflage properties, lending to its apotropaic attributions.

When first cut, the alder sap bleeds from the grain causing the wood to turn a deep orange red, this in turn led to several superstitions being associated with alder. To cut an alder without reason was to wound a living spirit, and yet in its bleeding the alder demonstrates its apotropaic powers as a being that wards off evil influences by reflecting or absorbing it. For the Celts the alder wood burned so ferociously that it was utilised to forge the finest weapons and tools for trade. Not only does it burn brightly and strongly, when all water and other constituents are burnt away alder transforms into high quality carbonised charcoal. The powers of alder from a literal and figurative perspective exemplify the alchemical qualities of resistance and transformation. It is a tree that conceals and protects and holds within the potential for fire that changes all things it touches.

Aldar appears in another section of the Second Branch, albeit subtly and perhaps unnoticed by many. When Branwen is questioned by the Irish regarding the peculiar scene they have witnessed out at sea, they ask:

> *"Beth yw y coet a welat ar y mor?" heb wy. "Gwernenni llongeu a hwylbrenni." heb hi.*[28]
> "What is the forest that was seen on the ocean?"
> "They are the alder-masts of the ships and sail trees."
> Said Branwen.

A deeper mystery is revealed when we compare the above with other references to alder within the Welsh tradition. In the *Book of Taliesin,* a collection of poetry attributed to be in the voice of the prototypic poet and prodigy of the Witch Goddess,

Cerridwen, we find the epic poem *Cad Goddeu* (The Battle of the Trees), where Gwydion summons and army of trees that is led by the Alder.

Gwern blaen llin, a want gysseuin.

Alder at the head of the line, struck first.

In a later poem, whose authenticity has been questioned by modern scholars, the alder appears again in direct relation to Brân:

These are the Englynion that were sung at the Cad Goddau, or as others have called it, the Battle of Achren which was because of the white roebuck and a welp, and they both came from Annwn, and Amaethon the son of Dôn brought them. And thereafter Amaethon the son of Dôn, and Arawn the King of Annwn fought. There was a man in that battle, unless his name were known he could not be overcome, and there was on the other side a woman called Achren, and unless her name were known her party could not be overcome. And Gwydion the son of Dôn guessed the name of the man and he sang the Englyn that follows:

"Sure-hoofed is my stallion impelled by the spur,
The high sprigs of alder are on your shield,
Brân is your name, of the glittering branches.

Sure hoofed is your stallion in the day of battle,
The high sprigs of alder are in your hand,
Bran by the branch that you bear,
Amaethon the good has prevailed."[29]

Whilst evidently connected in a manner that has been lost to a modern audience, they offer a tantalising glimpse at mystery for the polytheist. I propose that what is reflected here in the association between Brân, Branwen and Gwern is that they are presented as individual characters for narrative purposes only. What swims beneath is the mystery that they are not separate figures but rather represent the current of transformation that is expressed in three seemingly distinct, yet connected forms, Brân as the Bridge, Branwen as the Vessel and Gwern as the Flame. And yet it is the alder that stands at the heart of it all, the tree that bleeds like human flesh, the being that thrives in liminal places and burns ferociously to become the new fuel of creation, pure carbon. In the *Cad Goddeu*, it is alder that heads the army of trees, in the same manner that Brân leads his people across the sea, both represent the breaking open of the gates to the Otherworld and its influence. It is only by identifying the sprigs of alder on Brân's shield and hand that he can be named, he is named by the transformative powers of Gwern. These mysteries remind us that the deepest and most challenging of initiations is never about survival but transformation. Gwern represents the burning away of all false truths until only the truth of one's being remains.

Therefore, when Efnisien casts the boy into the fire of the House of a Hundred Columns, whilst seemingly devastating, we must pause to consider the power of myth; this is not simply a child that is being destroyed, but a symbolic gesture of casting alder into fire and thus activating its magical properties. This is no ordinary destruction, the burning of the child of alder can be perceived as an act of unveiling. It is the necessary release of illusion; it reveals a hidden truth that peace cannot be built upon pride and vengeance. Within the fires of the House of a Hundred Columns, Gwern transforms into the seed of wisdom, it highlights the cost of lost sovereignty and the unbearable heartbreak that forges deep and profound compassion.

Gwern as the Hidden Self

To be placed in accordance with the wisdom of Gwern, the polytheist must consider that the alder child represents a symbol of the hidden inner self, that part of the human soul that expresses vulnerability and transformation. Gwern is the inner child of the mythic psyche, it is the secret hope that is born from deep sorrow, but it is also the first to suffer when sorrow is supressed or denied which tears at the sovereignty of self. The myth is revealing to us a spiritual truth, that when we lose our innocence, we must then pass through the fires of consciousness. What remains after the intense fires resembles the power of alder charcoal to transmute pain into wisdom.

Through the message of Gwern we learn that what is submerged is never truly lost, and what is cast into the fires of transformation is never wholly destroyed. Beneath the surface and beyond the radiant flames the roots of alder endure. Through the mysteries of Gwern we learn that the human soul, akin to the alder becomes strongest when it stands within the tumultuous waters of sorrow and reaches for the light that resides within. Gwern is positioned where the human and divine realms intersect, it is the child of Branwen, daughter of the sea-god, and of Matholwch King of the proxy Otherworld. Gwern's brief life and violent death reminds us that when human and divine forces meet, anabolism and catabolism coexist within that moment, and their power can destroy or lead to transformation.

If we turn our attention momentarily to Efnisien, his actions might be his ultimate transgression, but it also carries a deeper, yet tragic insight. The power of Efnisien as the embodiment of the shadow, the human spider-sense, should never be underestimated for he perceives that the peace between the two islands is hollow and insincere. The meeting at the House of the Hundred Columns is based upon false foundations and acts as a political disguise to mask a deep betrayal. His actions destroy the illusion of unity and burn away falsehood to reveal truth.

From a narrative perspective we must also consider that Gwern is the rightful heir to the throne of Ireland, and his destruction destabilises the sovereignty of the entire nation. The peace that should have been born of Branwen's sufferings cannot survive deceit; it must all be undone so that the deeper wound can finally be acknowledged. Her subsequent heartbreak and death from sorrow is the completion of this devastating cycle of events. Through the loss of her child, Branwen becomes more than a Queen and sister of the King of Britain, she too is transformed by the fires of Gwern into the embodiment of collective grief, her four-sided grave on the banks of the River Alaw sings of the soul of a nation that is broken apart by its own violence and loss of sovereignty.

The Cry of Morddwyd Tyllion

As Gwern is cast into the fire, the balance of worlds collapses, the result in not merely a war between humans, but the unravelling of the sacred order. Amidst this chaos, we hear a strange voice that cries out from the madness:

> *Gwern gwngwch uiwch Vordwyt Tyllyon!*[30]
> Hounds of Gwern, beware of Morddwyd Tyllion!

This striking phrase is peculiar for it echoes like a riddle from the deep past. The name Morddwyd Tyllion means 'the pierced thigh', a wounding that has long been associated with sovereignty and fertility. This is the same wound that is borne by the Fisher King in later Arthurian tradition, where the wellbeing of the chosen King reflects the health and vitality of the land. The cry of Morddwyd Tyllion is not merely that of a desperate man in the throes of battle, it is instead the cry of wounded kingship, the lament of order that has lost its centre.[31] Who then are the hounds of Gwern? To the polytheist they may be understood as the unadulterated forces of the Otherworld being unleashed.

Once the alder is burnt the liminal border between this world and the other immediately disintegrates and those in battle become insane beasts driven by a wild instinct and tumultuous rage. The Hounds of Gwern represent the blind impulses of the human condition that rush forward when innocence has been cruelly destroyed. No longer the child that represents peace to stabilise unruly forces, what remains is the pack of our own ungoverned emotions. The cry of Morddwyd Tyllion is the wounded self that is shouting out into the maelstrom, seeking to hold its sovereignty amidst the chaos of emotion.

Within this dreadful moment, myth becomes a mirror for the human condition. It exemplifies what happens when our compassion and innocence are utterly consumed by the intense fires of our own making. Within each of us we all carry a Gwern, that part of us that is liminal and strives for harmony, to bridge the realms of land, water and sky, to understand the power of fire that is created by the interaction of the three realms. When our inner Gwern is cast into the flames, the Hounds are unleashed, and through inappropriate responses to sorrow and grief we might easily move towards vengeance of the unhealed heart. Amidst the ashes of alder, deep within the waters of sorrow and the hardened heart, Gwern has one final lesson to offer, new shoots and transformation is always possible. Sovereignty that is lost is not a finality, it can be reborn, but for its rebirth to occur we must acknowledge the Hounds that may arise from that wounding and cease feeding them, moving instead towards tending the wounds that initially damaged us.

Thus, as is common in the *Mabinogi*, the cry of Morddwyd Tyllion is not one of desperation or despair, but rather a warning. The cry reminds us that when innocence dies, we must take great caution and care in attending to that which might rise in its place. The Hounds of Gwern represent elements of our own shadow and hurt; to quell the cry we must, therefore, reclaim the kingship that lies within us.

The Hidden Mystery of the Mother of Alder

And so, at the conclusion of our journey with alder, we must once again return to Branwen herself. As the narrative falls into chaos, we are offered another peculiar statement that is worthy of note and examination:

> *Ac yn yd aeth pawb ym pen yr arueu, y hynhelis Bendigeiduran Uranwen y rwng y taryan a'y yscwyd.*[32]
> As each went for his weapons, Bendigeidfran held Branwen between his shield and his shoulder.[33]

On the surface this appears to be an act of protection. Brân's shield is an obvious symbol of defence whereas his shoulder is the place of bearing burdens. In holding his sister in this position, he is proclaiming that he will guard her, and he will carry her. Brân as the giant King shelters the broken feminine principle and her heart of peace between his warfare and his humanity. The shield represents his outer defence and his shoulder his inner strength. In that space Branwen is offered a moment of sanctuary amidst the descent into chaos. What we are witnessing in this short line is a representation of the reconciliation of masculine protection with feminine sorrow, it is a moment of compassion that arises from all that is being wounded around them. Even as their world descends into war, Brân's immediate instinct is not hellbent on vengeance but rather on guardianship.

Further mystery can be gleaned when we consider another statement within the Second Branch. Branwen is named as one of the three chief *rieni* of the islands of Britain. The middle Welsh term *rieni* is rendered as *rhieni* in modern Welsh, meaning parent or parents. And yet in its Middle Welsh meaning it can be used figurately to represent ancestor/s.[34] But this presents a peculiarity, for how can Branwen be a chief ancestor parent if she bore only one child, and that child was killed? What then can be meant by referring to her as a chief ancestress? Herein lies the mystery, for her lineage is not one of the flesh, but rather of the spirit. Branwen is our ancestral mother, not through blood but instead through the experience of shared sorrow and the intense burning that each of us must sometimes endure to become our whole and authentic selves again. As a child of Branwen, the alder within us, that deep and hidden part of the soul that may be burned is also renewed by her mystery. She is the one that holds us when we emerge from the flames, changed, our grief and sorrows transformed into wisdom, our despair transmuted into compassion.

Branwen's role as a *rieni* implies a compassion that is born from suffering, she is the great parent of endurance, the ancestor of those who have felt they have lost everything and yet have retained their humanity. Essentially, Branwen gives birth to understanding rather than a dynasty as implied in the narrative. Through her endurance and dignity, we as her descendants of story and spirit inherit her wisdom born of sorrow. She is indeed our rieni, the ancestral mother of the human soul, she teaches us that true sovereignty is not the avoidance of sorrow, but our ability to walk through its tenacious flames and emerge transformed. Essnetially we are all Gwern, the child of transformation, in sufferance of occasional sorrow, but shaped by endurance and resilience. If given a human voice, she would ask us to consider that we do not flee from the fires of apparent destruction but instead move towards understanding what it burns away and no longer serves us.

Chapter 9

The Sovereignty of Sorrow – Finding the Sacred in Loss

Having explored the many facets of Branwen and her family that this short book allows, it will soon be time to move towards developing a practise. But before I venture into offering you exercise and rituals of connection, it feels fitting to explain why I am choosing a particular facet of Branwen to explore rather than the many attributes she embodies. In many ways Branwen has walked beside me throughout my entire life, I knew of her even when I was a young child growing up in the mountains of North Wales. In my adult life her presence was always there, a quiet stillness, a whispering song that accompanied me during my career as an autopsy technologist and bereavement officer. Initially her song came as the tortured breath between the sobs of the grieving, echoing through the corridors of the morgue. She was present in the hush that follows the final heartbeat, and she rose in the screams of despair of those caught in the maelstrom of loss.

Even as a professional, there are times when words serve no purpose or meaning, that silence and presence is enough to offer the bereaved. In those moments I could sense her, a quiet grace that holds the bereaved, the dead and the living alike, a mute dignity that does not flee from sorrow. In essence, Branwen has always been the stillness at the centre of my world, she has been my unseen companion in my service to the dead and the bereaved. Therefore, it makes sense to me, as I hope it does to you, that this is the thread that I chose to follow, for it aligns with my own sense of self-sovereignty. This is not to suggest that she does not express other attributes equally worthy of exploration, for she does. To some they may connect to her as those who are themselves calumniated, others because they have been silenced. To some she is a sea-born goddess that sings of our inexorable connection to the Otherworld, however we may perceive it. As the peacemaker she teaches us the art of reconciliation and the delicate balance that exists between forgiveness and righteousness. As the bird whisperer she carries messages between the living and the dead, she acts as a conduit between memory and forgetting. As the weaver of souls, she spins each broken thread of the heart into wisdom. Each of these facets is true, each valuable and worthy of connection.

It would appear disingenuous of me to ponder over all of these and offer you, the reader a way in which to explore all of them, when the way she reveals herself to me is as the sovereign of sorrow, the weaver of loss. In essence, Branwen is a prism, the fracturing of light into its different spectrums, so too do her attributes sing to each of us in a different manner, one that is unique to our own lived experience and in concordance with our sovereignty.

In my many years of dealing with and working with the dead and the bereaved, I have come to learn that grief is not merely one emotion, but rather a kingdom of emotions that express different landscapes of loss. The sovereign task in all this is not to attempt to control them, they are after all a necessary component of the human condition, the price we pay for love is the pain of loss. In connecting with Branwen, she teaches us not by offering comfort or moving towards vanquishing the pain, but instead she asks us to hold our pain with reverence and honour. She asks us to consider that true sovereignty is not a gleaming crown, and neither is it a throne; it is our capacity to be fully present when our hearts are torn apart.

When we give grief and loss the ear that they demand, by not pushing it away, or medicating ourselves with the mundane, we slowly discover a quiet and indestructible centre that resides within ourselves. Within her story we may come to the realisation that even when our world burns to ashes, and the heart explodes into a red mist that something sacred remains. An echo of the love that once filled that space, and when we find that we continue to have the capacity to love, to care, to be compassionate and empathetic we bear witness to the inherent power of our humanity. This is the sovereignty of sorrow; it is that which endures the collapse of relationships and the breaking of hearts.

We are the inheritors of myth, they live within us, not only as echoes of distant gods that have morphed through time, but as mirrors in which we can see reflected the hidden structures of our own lives. Branwen asks us to consider that grief is not a fall from the spiritual path, it is the path itself. Our broken hearts become the Cauldron, the very vessel in which wisdom is brewed. When perceived from this perspective the Cauldron becomes the heart itself, the vessel that is warmed by love, stirred by loss, and transformed by the wisdom of time. The sea, which is her kin, represents the vast and sometimes tumultuous currents of feeling that move through each of us. As corvid she is the witness, the divine messenger of transformation who teaches us that endings and beginnings are intimately connected.

Branwen whispers to us that whilst our sovereignty may be diminished by sorrow and grief, they do not herald the end of sovereignty but rather its refinement.

When we move into relationship with Branwen we learn to walk the path of grief as a process of sacred initiation. Whilst it can discombobulate us, Branwen offers a space in which we can emotionally relocate that which has been lost, allowing it to settle and find a home within us. In her company we can learn that the sufferance of sorrow is not a wound from which we can be fully healed but acts as a teacher that we learn to honour. We can never be the same person we were before loss, but we can find ways in which our sovereignty may rise like a phoenix from the mythic flames and therein honour that which we have endured as an aspect of the song of our living.

When we find meaning in myth, we may become that which Branwen embodies, the healer of souls, not by medication or avoidance, but as our new and authentic selves that rise from heartbreak. She teaches us that love, despite its cost is always worthwhile.

Branwen and the Power of Place
Sacred Landscape of Loss and Renewal

Branwen is intimately connected to the land of Wales, in particularly Ynys Môn (The Isle of Anglesey), the legendary chief seat of the British Druids of the Iron Age. She does not exist in isolation, she is interwoven with the fabric of the land that gave up these stories for humans to interpret and tell in their own words, using cultural keys to embellish them. Stories are the way in which humankind make sense of their place in the world, their power to enchant us continues to this day. They are indicative of the history of the heart, not that written by the ulterior motives of the conqueror or the coloniser but rise from the ethereal connection that a people have to their land.

Branwen is not merely a mythic figure but an archetype that sings of the land itself. The land remembers, its hills and rivers, brooks and streams, holy wells and springs, ancient trees that stand as sentinels to the passing of time are not silent witnesses, but living and inspirited archives, these are the keepers of story of song that sing to the hearts of the Bards and storytellers. It is important that we consider that the *Mabinogi* is not simply an abstract collection of myths that have taken wing to inspire the world, they are simultaneously an expression of the voice of the land. Each myth contains a silver thread that is tethered to the geography from which they were born, each one pulses within the body of the land.

Branwen's tale is intimately rooted in the sacred landscape of the Isle of Anglesey, a gleaming jewel floating in the Irish sea, the ancient homeland of the Druids and their sovereignty over the islands of Britain and Northern Europe. Their sovereignty was usurped by the coming of Rome, and whilst the echo of that sorrow remains within the foundations of this land and our culture, we have found ways to be healed and renewed, to reclaim our sovereignty.

Bedd Branwen – The Four-Sided Grave of Branwen

On the banks of the River Alaw in the quiet, windswept fields of central Anglesey there lies a low ancient burial cairn of stones, known as *Bedd Branwen* (The Grave of Branwen), within the Second Branch we are told:

> *guae ui o'm ganedigaeth. Da a dwy ynys a diffeithwyt o'm achaws i. A dodi ucheneit uawr, a thorri y chalon ar hynny. A gwneuthur bed petrual idi, a'e cladu yno yglan Alaw.*[35]
> Woe that I was every born, two good islands have been laid to waste because of me. She gave a great sigh, and with that her heart breaks. And they made for her a four-sided grave and buried her there on the banks of the Alaw.

From an archaeological perspective the site has long been referred to as Ynys Branwen (the Island of Branwen), albeit the site is significantly earlier than the eventual penning of the *Mabinogi*, she is none the less intimately connected to this place. The Bronze Age ring cairn is topped by a mighty stone that has been weathered by centuries of wind and rain, it takes the form of a heart, one that is split cleanly down the middle. It appears from above as the image of a broken heart as if cleaved in two by the powers of grief, and it may be this peculiarity that gave rise to the story or to Branwen's association with this place. It stands there still as a symbol of enduring love and sorrow. Its fracture sings of her story, and yet the heart endures, it has not crumbled into dust but rather bears its wound with a grace akin to Branwen. It is not a symbol of despair, but of compassion, the stone heart has been split wide enough to contain the grief of the world. It stands today as a powerful place of pilgrimage to connect to the quiddity of Branwen.

Deep within the ring cairn and covered by flag stones a space was discovered that contained pottery urns, each one turned upside-down, full of ashes from cremated remains. Within these urns were discovered several sets of perfectly intact infant bones from the human inner ear. The malleus, incus and stapes bones are incredibly small, their extraction from the human skull would have been a painstaking procedure. Why would the ancestors have gone to such trouble to extract them? When we consider the function of these bones, they form a bridge between vibration and hearing, between the invisible world of sound and the conscious act of listening. Whether or not the ancestors understood this function can never be truly known, but from a mythic perspective they provide a connection to the attributes of Branwen. These tiny bones are the gatekeepers of perception. We might consider that their intentional positioning within the tomb is an acknowledgment that the sense of hearing continues after death, and that the ancestors continue to listen to the living world.

This offers a beautiful symbolic correlation with Branwen's story, for her tragedy begins when she is not heard, when her cries go unnoticed. The entire catastrophic events of the Second Branch unfold from a failure to listen. The discovery of ear bones at Bedd Branwen might represent a restoration of sacred hearing, where we acknowledge that through death and grief, beyond the silence of the grave, that sacred listening might be restored. For me, it feels like the land on the banks of the River Alaw has taken these bones into its sacred keeping, offering the promise and affirmation to hear that which has been previously ignored. Whilst the presence of these bones is odd, I find that they are profoundly fitting. They represent the continuation of communication between the living and the dead. Within the context of the grave and Branwen's story they may hold the power of atonement, where we strive to restore right hearing with integrity and compassion between the broken halves of hearts.

Through Branwen's teachings we learn that to hear is to heal, that when we listen deeply to the currents of our own being and of those around us, pain can be transformed into understanding. And from that understanding we move into the currents of the land itself and begin to write new lyrics to the sacred music that connects us to the voice of the land. Another truth arises from this, that myths are not something to be merely read, but something to be heard, through the ears, through the land itself, and through that quiet voice that resides in each of us that is singing us back to wholeness.

The Stone Heart and the River

The stone heart reminds me of the nature of alder when submerged in water, it becomes as stone, perpetual, unmoving, a silent witness to the passage of time, a reminder to the living of the power of permanence. The four-sided grave in which Branwen is buried can represent the cosmology of the Celtic world where four expresses wholeness, order and completion. It is connected to the four winds, the four directions and we might also consider it in relation to the Four Branches of the *Mabinogi*. Branwen's grave is not simply a tomb but is instead a cosmic enclosure, a place where the sorrows of her life and teachings are reconciled with the harmony of the land. We will never know what came first, the tomb or the myth, the myth or the tomb, but in this place, there is a tangibility to her story, it provides a space in which we can sense the intimate connection between myth and land. It is a place of solace and contemplation, to arrive at Bedd Branwen is to walk into a space that expresses a peculiar emptiness, too much of an emptiness for not to have been full only moments before. It asks us to ponder what we see, what we hear and what the heart feels.

Windswept and barren, the mound of Bedd Branwen lies adjacent to the River Alaw, the word Alaw in Welsh means music, a piece of music, air, tune, melody.[36] The name of the river literally translates as the River of Music and Song. The waters of the Alaw carouse through the landscape of the Isle of Anglesey, eventually meeting the sea at Aber Alaw (The Estuary of Alaw) in the northwestern corner of the island. Rivers are liminal thresholds, the life blood of the land, and this one is intimately connected to song and music, it serves to remind us that Branwen's story has not concluded, it flows on to this day, like the perpetual flowing river that surrounds her grave. Know the mystery, there is not a single drop of new water on our planet, each drop has existed in a billion forms, travelled through billions of expressions of life. Each drop carries the memories of all that it has encountered. If we consider this mystery, the river Alaw continues to carry the song and memory of Branwen, it carries her sorrow, her grief, wisdom and love through time upon its gentle currents. To stand on the banks of the Alaw is to stand in her presence, to hear her mysteries whispering to the hearts of those who are willing to listen. In the same manner that the waters of the Alaw enrich the land around it, her wisdom nourishes the souls of those who connect with her.

The grave and the river provide us with an opportunity for pilgrimage, to stand in the living landscape that birthed the myths. But the waters of the river disseminate her wisdom to the world, for all rivers carry this wisdom; all rivers are connected one to the other through the hydrological system. There is much power in pilgrimage, to sacrifice time and effort to visit a location for spiritual succour. However, any moving body of water provides an opportunity to connect with Branwen, regardless of where we are on the earth. The key to connection is simple, it is reflected in the name of the river, Alaw, to stand on its banks or any other river and call to Branwen, I suggest that you do so in song, with melody and rhythm. This simple but powerful act transforms the mythic landscape, for the river is the flowing current of sound itself.

In Welsh cosmology and particularly within the Bardic tradition, the divine connection between air, song and spirit is everything, the term *ysbryd* (spirit) is etymologically connected to the Latin term *spiritus* meaning vitality of breath. They are inseparable, they express deep mystery that we can all access through our lungs. Branwen's presence is accessed through air and song. To sing is to offer our vulnerability, to give of ourselves, it can become the vehicle through which grief and sorrow can be expressed and subsequently transmuted, it is the *alaw* through which our sorrow can find its sovereignty. When we sing in her honour, we allow sorrow to find its voice, when we breathe with intention, we move closer to her mythic currents and may be carried by the *alaw*, the divine melody of healing and remembrance. Through this teaching we can move to understand that a relationship with Branwen cannot arise from intellectual understanding alone, it must come from embodied expression, from having the courage to allow your emotions to move as currents of air, as song.

Within the Welsh language, the term for song or to sing is *cân* with verb being *canu*, however, the term does not distinguish a cân as lyrical, musical singing alone.[37] A cân may also be a recited piece of poetry with its meter and rhyme being rhythmic and akin to musical singing. Singing a popular song or reciting a poem are both considered to be acts of singing.

In truth and vulnerability, it is through my grief and my work with the dead and bereaved that I came to develop an intimate relationship with Branwen. Her story has become a mirror to my own experience, a visceral echo of what it means to love, to lose but to rise again holding the fragments of my own broken heart, and the hearts of others as sacred fragments of relationship. And thus, my connection to her is not abstract and neither is it purely mythical, it is lived and felt through the continuous work of tending to grief and sorrow. It is this perspective that I hope to offer you, the reader, that as you reach towards Branwen you will learn and understand that even in the breaking of hearts the melodious song of life continues to flow.

Within the pages of this short introduction to Branwen we have travelled across mythic waters, but it is now time to turn our attention inward, from understanding to embodiment. In the following chapter I offer you ways in which you can develop a relationship with Branwen, through ritual, magic and other exercises, and practises that allow grief to be transformed into grace, and for loss to reveal its hidden gifts of sovereignty.

Chapter 10

The Cauldron of the Heart – Embodying Branwen's Blessings

The keys to any successful and meaningful connection with a non-human spirit, are intention and integrity. Humans embody the qualities and attributes of spiritual principles when they express their virtues in their own lives. The following practises are designed to help you discover Branwen's virtues and to move closer to her energetic spectrum.

Of important note is the nature of how deity interacts with the world of humanity. For those who have not been fortunate enough to have been raised in polytheistic communities, which amounts to most people in the Western World, a shift in perspective is necessary. For many westerners, especially those over the age of 40, our initial programming came from a monotheistic mindset and worldview. This subtle influence cannot be overestimated, for it bleeds into the fabric of our experience of the numinous. When we move on from monotheism and encounter polytheism, our concepts of the divine will be intricately woven into the mechanism of monotheistic belief. Therefore, for many who are new to contemporary western Pagan practise, their concept of the divine may be strikingly like that of the over-culture. This is a difficult pattern to break, simply because we were not raised to perceive more than one deity, and for modern polytheists we are attempting to find our feet beneath the table of polytheism.

Whilst Branwen and her kin may well be euhemerised deities from the distant past, there is no evidence that a cult or shrine was ever established using the names Branwen and Brân. This does not negate the function of them being deities in the 21st century. Within myth, they are not referred to as gods, but rather as royal figures in the lineage of the sea god, Llŷr.

However, when peered at through a looking glass, we can see as this book has demonstrated that their myth is unmistakenly interwoven with the language of divinity. Themes of giants, talking heads, magical cauldrons and supernatural occurrences pepper the stories. They are evidently not ordinary mortals, instead they are the echoes of gods that have been clothed in the colourful garments of history.

Defining the shift from deity to mythical figure is not easy, and neither does it lessen them, instead it transforms them. The aim of this book was not one of reanimating a long-forgotten goddess, but rather to recognise elements of the divine that never truly disappear, but that are transmuted by relationship. By process of apotheosis, the spiritual principle of the divine rises again, but in a new form. It is of no consequence if the ancient Celts recognised the names Brân and Branwen as gods, what is important is that we recognise that their qualities have been embodied in us, in this time. To understand this, we must consider the earlier truth that whilst the myths and the figures they contain have an ancient element, they are also timeless. I reiterate, the spiritual principle embodied in these figures is simultaneously ancient and timeless, immanent and imminent. The immanency of the gods transcends time and place; they sing from the virtues that they embody; their imminency is exemplified in their arrival into this moment. For when we speak, write, sing or express them by whatever means, they imminently arrive within the immanency of the moment.

Contrary to some popular claims over the past several decades of pagan writing, the Welsh myths are not records of an ancient faith. Wales, its language and culture are alive, it evolves and develops continuously, in this same manner the subjects of this book continue to reveal themselves to us. By means of euhemerization the old gods entered the living world of story and myth, by processes of apotheosis they rise again within us. When we take this to heart, we come to understand that

Branwen is not a relic of an ancient belief system, she is a living presence that is rediscovered through those who are willing to listen. Therefore, when we move into relationship with the spirit of Branwen, we are not engaging in reviving an old religion, neither are we reconstructing something from the deep past. We are moving into meaningful and sincere relationship with the quiddity of the divine that has endured for millennia, through hundreds of different names. These mysteries have been held deep in our own cultural memory, and it is through the voices of modern polytheists that they once again rise into song, one that is appropriate and applicable to modernity.

We will commence the practises that follow by addressing the issues mentioned above, by moving with intention into the stream of polytheistic thinking. Moving one's perspective from a monotheist to a polytheist mindset is not about abandonment and rejection, but rather about widening our circle of understanding to accommodate voices that may have been silenced but never stopped singing. We do not adopt polytheism, it is a way of noticing, and of entering relationality with the divine that moves through all things.

Exercise 1.
Opening the Spirit to the Many – Reawakening Sacred Conversation

I suggest that the following exercise be performed if you are new to the concept of polytheism, but to those have been treading this path for some time, it may also be helpful. Whilst this version includes the name and virtues of Branwen, it can be adapted for any deity.

Take to a quiet space where you will not be disturbed and have in the centre of that space a single candle. To the left position a symbol that reflects your previous spiritual or religious upbringing or faith. It may be a religious icon, or a symbol drawn onto paper. If you came from no faith or atheism, a blank page would accurately represent this. To the right place an icon or symbol to represent polytheism, perhaps a triskele or a sequence of small circles orbiting a larger circle. Use your imagination and connection.

Take a deep breath, one for the land, one for the sea and one for the sky, light the candle and allow your breath to settle. Let your awareness drop consciously from your head to your heart. Fix your gaze on your chosen symbol to the left of the candle for several minutes, allowing its meaning to fall into your heart. Next cast your gaze to the symbol on the left and do the same. Finally bring your eyes to focus on the candle flame, with the two symbols in the periphery of your vision. The flame is the bridge between them.

Consider the mechanism and situations that have caused this shift in your perspective, breathing deeply as you do.

Place your hands, palms down over the symbols you have chosen and repeat the following words or those of your own choosing:

I was taught that God was one, afar,
A distant light, a lonely star.
Now I hear a thousand names,
Each one ablaze with sacred flames.
My heart is open to the many who sing,
Through wind and water, by wave and wing,
Through stories of sorrow, by silence and song,
Voices who whispered my name to belong.
To Branwen I open, O weaver of pain,
The healer of hearts made whole again.
You teach that holiness falls with tears,
And love is reborn when the heart appears.
Allow me to learn with wonder's grace,
To see the divine in every face.

To walk with courage, to sense and explore,
For the gods are within me, and I am their door.

Repeat the above or similar as often as you feel comfortable, allowing the words to ripple through you. As you fall into silence imagine that the light of the candle casts a bridge of illumination between the chosen symbols. Consider the following questions:

- What if the divine is not somewhere else, but rather here in this moment and moving through all things?
- What is the divine is not separate from creation, or superior to it, but rather an expression of it?
- How do the virtues of the gods express themselves through my life?
- What if I do not need to believe differently, but rather only listen differently?

In the silence that follows, sit quietly and place your power hand (the one you write with) over your heart and repeat this affirmation:

May I remember, both gentle and strong,
That I am the sacred, a part of its song.

Sit in further silence and when ready extinguish the candle, remove the symbols returning them to their home, or burn them if on paper.

Exercise 2
Moving into the Currents of Branwen

The following ritual is designed to assist you into moving into awareness of Branwen's virtues and energies, calling her gently to engage with you. For this ritual you will need:

- A plain white candle for purity and illumination.
- A small bowl or cauldron of water to represents Branwen's tears and the powers of the sea.
- A handful of Hawthorn berries or other plant material that represents the heart.

Take a few moments to centre yourself in your space and find stillness. Light the candle and repeat the following or similar words:

Branwen, I call upon your gentle tide,
Arise and come unto my side,
Upon the waves of joy and pain,
O daughter of Llŷr, I call your name
Branwen! Branwen! Branwen!

Now dip your fingers into the water and allow it to drip from your fingertips onto the surface of the palm of your other hand. Repeat the following or similar word:

O blessed Branwen,
Jackdaw of sorrow and compassion,
You have known the shores of loss,
Teach me the grace of your forgiveness,
The strength that rises from that which is broken,
The love that endures beyond all endings.
O daughter of Llŷr, I call your name.
Branwen! Branwen! Branwen!

Now take the Hawthorn berries or whatever item you have selected to represent the heart and place them before the bowl/cauldron of water and repeat the following words or similar:

As I give, so do I receive,
As I remember, so am I healed.

Branwen, weave your song into my life,
O daughter of Llŷr, come stand at my side,
Branwen! Branwen! Branwen!

Remain in quiet contemplation for several moments, allowing any sense of her presence to fall into your awareness. Be aware of a sense of stillness after tears, the calmness that often follows a storm, a sense of quiet reflection, a tugging at your emotional centre around your solar plexus. It is in these feelings that Branwen makes herself known to you.

Conclude this ritual by extinguishing the candle and as the smoke rises into the air say:

Blessed is your name, O Branwen,
Be with me now and ever dwell within my heart.

Keep the water and berries on your chosen space until you feel the time is right to offer them to the earth.

Exercise 3
Singing Through Symbology – Contemplating the Virtues of Branwen

Creating rituals and ceremonial processes to connect to the divine are powerful motivators and affirmation of relationality. But at times, simplicity is key. When we move towards the use of symbols, they can speak to the language of the soul in a way that is different to complex ritualistic practises. They allow for the unseen to communicate directly with the inner self. Symbols act as more than mere representations, they are vessels of immense power, the more we use them, the more powerful they become. They can speak directly to an ancient part of us that transcends logic.

The following sigil, created specifically for Branwen hold the qualities of her virtues in its patterns. By contemplating and meditating on her sigil, tracing its lines with a finger or placing it upon a sacred object or an item used in spell-crafting it allows her virtues to bypass the rational part of the human brain. In this manner the sigil becomes a mirror for the soul and a representation of the connection you have to Branwen.

You may use the following sigil, created specifically for her, or you may be moved to create one of your own choosing. Use your smart-device to photograph the sigil directly from this book or photocopy it to keep about your person and sacred spaces in your home. You may wish to replicate it and position it upon an altar or other space that expresses your connection to her.

When moved to do so, or in any working with Branwen, soften your breathing and focus on the sigil. You may wish to trace its pattern with a finger or a wand. As you do, allow the image to imprint itself on your mind so that you can easily recall it with your eyes closed. Within the stillness of your chosen space, and your focus on the sigil, repeat the following or similar words:

By this sigil I speak to you,
Heart split, wing of night,

Tears that fall by silver dew,
A binding thread to dark and light.

O Branwen, weaver of sorrow's art,
Teach me the grace of the broken heart,
Through loss and love, your truth is known,
What is torn apart, returns as stone. (repeat this section x3)

Upon the banks, where the Alaw flows,
Your name through its current goes,
O lady of the Corvid's call,
Lift my heart, though I may fall.

Remain in this space for some time or move onto any other working you have in mind with her.

Exercise 4
Bedd Branwen – the Four-Sided Altar

Altars offer a space in which we can consider and develop our relationship with the divine, they can be permanent or semi-permanent. Whilst the following ritual is designed to create a space in which any work with Branwen can be performed, it may also be adapted as an altar space (for this the items selected would need to be small enough to fit onto a table or shelf).

Otherwise, consider the items and their symbolic significance, collecting them carefully and placing them around your person, forming a four-sided grave that evokes that of Bedd Branwen.

This practise can be used for several reasons:

- To designate a space as sacred for the work ahead.
- To act as a focal point at the commencement of any ritual.

- To anchor her work within the human heart.
- As a grounding method that pulls on mythical themes.
- As an act of protection for the heart.
- To become a ritualist sacred container for any work your do in relation to her.
- To act as a space to honour her virtues as they are reflected in your emotional landscape.
- To allow one to release the burden of pain into a space where it can be honoured and assimilated into experience.

Choose four symbols to represent the four sides of Bedd Branwen:

- *North* – a stone of your choosing or a heart formed of clay to represent endurance, resilience and permanence.
- *East* – a corvid feather or small cauldron for incense or an incense holder and stick to represent the power of song and the cry of the corvids.
- *South* – a candle of your choosing to represent the burning and transformation of Gwern.
- *West* – a small bowl or cauldron of naturally sourced water to represent the River Alaw, the flow of tears and remembrance.

Arrange these items around your working space or replicate them in miniature if creating a more permanent altar for your work. Arrange the items with purpose and intent, calling their attributions in your own words as you position them.

Stand or sit at the centre, or hold your hands over the items if positioned on an altar, and repeat the following or similar:

Four sides of your grave now hold me,
Four winds of feeling now bless me,

In your name, O Branwen,
Blessed heart of sorrow, I am made whole.

After allowing the stillness of the moment to arrive fully, you may move onto your primary focus, using the above as an establishing ritual for any appropriate working with Branwen.

Exercise 5
The Ritual of the Broken Heart

Silently sitting adjacent to the River Alaw, the split heart shaped stone of Bedd Branwen is an evocative symbol of her story and mysteries. Whilst it may be tempting to believe that this is a defeatist symbol, on the contrary, it lies as cry to transformation for a broken heart is not empty, it is open to be filled again.

Heartache and heartbreak are aspects of the human condition that tie each one of us through pain, longing and loss. There are times when it is cathartic to name these things, not to vanquish them or to even lessen their power over us, but to honour them as vital aspects of the experience of living and loving.

For this ritual you will need a piece of natural air-drying clay, available from the banks of natural rivers or pre-packaged at a craft supply store. Warm the clay in your hands and slowly shape it to form a stylised heart. Use a craft tool, the end of a pen or a sharp fingernail to create a substantial and irregular line from the middle centre of the heart to the bottom. Hold it against your chest and whisper the names of the griefs you carry. Allow your words to come from the heart, revealing currents of emotion that need to be acknowledge.

Place the clay heart on an altar or other sacred space and allow to dry fully for approximately three days, depending on the size and density of the object. Return to it and holding it back against your heart, whisper to it again and note if your expression of emotions has changed to remain largely unchanged. Then, take the heart in both hands and break it in half, as you do repeat the following or similar words:

From brokenness, wholeness is born,
From sorrow, sovereignty arises.

Place the two halves of the heart on your Branwen altar or other sacred space, or if you wish, return it to dissolve in natural running water. As you do this, know the mystery, that your grief, longing, pain or sorrow is not lost to the wider world, but instead, becomes a part of the currents of life that flows through all things.

Exercise 6
A Ritual for Honouring Grief and Loss

Bereavement and loss can easily disarm and discombobulate, leaving one feeling literally beside oneself. The following ritual is not designed to vanquish or remove the pain and sorrow or loss, but rather to sit consciously within its currents, providing space for emotional relocation to occur. When we honour our grief, we allow it to settle within us and transform us, providing it with the space it needs to allow us to move gently towards healing and reconnection.

For this ritual you will need the following items:

- A white candle to represent Branwen.
- The sigil provided to you in Exercise 3.
- A corvid feather, or a black feather if you are unable to locate one, to represent Branwen's connection to the Corvid kin.
- A small bowl or cauldron of natural water.

- One small pebble or stone that can easily fit in the palm of your hand with your fingers wrapped around it.
- A journal and pen.
- A small nosegay or collection of flowers that evoke loss, lilies, lavender, marigolds.

Instructions:

- Take to the space of your choosing and prepare it according to your own practise or tradition. Candles and incense may be used to add atmosphere.
- Arrange the items listed on an altar or small table designated for sacred purpose.
- Position the candle in the centre of the space and arrange the remaining items in a manner that pleases you. Place the sigil directly before the candle and sit in quiet consideration of its meaning. Light the central candle and ground yourself into the space. Take three deep breaths, one with the land, one with the sky and one with the sea.
- Place your hands either side of the candle flame, feelings its warmth and call to the spirit of Branwen:

O Branwen, weaver of sorrows and healer of souls, I call upon you now. You have known the deepest currents of grief, the heaviest of losses, I ask that your spirit fills this space. I come seeking your guidance at this time of loss, I ask that you help me to weave my sorrows into grace, allowing my heart to find healing. O Branwen, I ask that you arise and come unto me.

- Now take the feather in the hand that you write with and hold it before the candle. The birds of Branwen act as messengers, taking her message across the turbulent seas. In the same manner the feather symbolically allows us to send our sorrows as an offering to her. Repeat the following or similar:

Branwen, as you sent your starling across the waves, carrying the burdens of your sorrow, so too do I send my sorrows as an offering to you. Allow me to release the weight that they place upon my soul, help me find peace within this journey of loss.

- Next, take the pebble or stone and hold it in your left hand, close your fingers around it, feeling its weight and texture in your hand. Imagine that this stone represents the weight of your grief and loss, allowing it to weigh as heavy as your heart feels. Pause to consider that which has been lost, allow yourself to feel the emotions that arise without attempting to steer or direct them.

When you feel ready say the following or similar words:

O Branwen, I hold in my hand the weight of my grief and sorrow. Teach me to carry this with wisdom and grace, to find a way to honour what has been and to create a space for that which will come.

Remain in this position, with the stone in your hand for several minutes. When the time feels right, release the stone into the bowl or cauldron of water. Imagine that the water softens the weight of your grief, without removing it. When you feel ready say the following words or similar:

I gift my sorrow to the silent waters of the soul. As Branwen's tears once fell, so too may my tears honour that which is lost, by water and earth may it be heard, and may it be transformed. I honour this gift of sorrow.

- Sit quietly for some time and allow the presence of this ritual and the spirits of Branwen to integrate into experience. Feel her presence as a gentle companion guiding you through the currents of grief.
- In time, note your impressions of the ritual into a journal whilst considering the following – *how can I honour this loss whilst continuing to move forward with my life? What message might Branwen have for me in this moment?*
- When the time feels right, bring the ritual to a close. Consider the items you have used and with the flowers in hand, offer a prayer of gratitude to Branwen for having been in this space with you:

Branwen, great queen of sorrow and transformation, sovereign of the heart I offer you, my gratitude. In this place I honour you as the weaver of sorrows, as healer of souls. May your wisdom and grace guide me as I continue to navigate the paths of my own pain.

- Extinguish the candle, allowing the memory of its light and warmth to carry the intentions of this ritual. Leave the stone in the water overnight, offering it the time it requires to allow the energies of the ritual to continue to work. Pour the water on the earth and carry the stone with you as a reminder of the power of ritual and the weight of your pain.
- You may repeat this ritual periodically as you continue your path of assimilation and transformation.

Conclusion

The Continuing Song of Branwen

We have travelled far in this short book, across the turbulent seas from which Branwen was born, to the shores of the Otherworld and the turrets of the Tower of London, we have soared with the cries of corvids and faced the presence of other sacred animals that have accompanied our journey. But her story cannot be contained within the pages of one short book, and neither can it be expressed fully within a single understanding of who she is. She is a tapestry of mystery clothed in feathers and tears. Her mysteries are as calm and turbulent as the waters of Llŷr, they are sometimes gentle and but also fierce and unpredictable. But in their perpetual movement they reflect something of the deep landscape of our own souls.

The words you have read here are the threads of one weaver's loom, they are drawn from my own experiences, from my personal grief and loss. They are not the only threads, nor are they meant to be as such. Instead, the words of this book are an invitation for you to lean deeper into the landscape of your own heart, to move closer to the ever-flowing energies of Branwen that swim at the core of the human experience.

There are as many ways to walk with Branwen as there are expressions of the human heart, your task is to navigate yours with grace and wisdom. My hope is that this work will act as a beginning and not as an end of your journey with her. Branwen's story never ends; it finds countenance and meaning in the many ways that hearts are broken and fill up again. Her song sings through your life, through mine and in all the ways that make us painfully but beautifully human. We honour her and her story when we open our hearts to a wisdom that is forged from sorrow and a love that never ceases to be expressed. May this work, open your being to the song of Branwen, weaver of sorrows and healer of souls.

Endnotes

1. I have intentionally chosen to use the name Brân as opposed to his full title 'Bendigeidfran', purely because this is the name I work with in my own spirituality. Both terms are correct within the Welsh tradition of Bardism and storytelling.
2. Williams. PKM. P xlii-xiv.
3. Bromwich. TYP. 418-420.
4. Annwfn is the older spelling, in modernity it may also be rendered as Annwn, both versions are correct.
5. Bromwich. TYP. 303-304.
6. Bromwich, TYP. 305-306.
7. Williams. PKM xxiii.
8. Original text from Llyfr Gwyn Rhyedderch.
9. Common English translation by the author.
10. https://welsh-dictionary.ac.uk/gpc/gpc.html
11. In the original manuscript the modern term Harlech is rendered as Hardlech, meaning the beautiful stone/rock.
12. Tolstoy. OBPL. 107.
13. Bromwich. TYP. 50.
14. Williams. PKM. P39.
15. See, Haycock. LPBOT.
16. The primary Cauldron of the Otherworld is capitalized to differentiate it from a cooking vessel.
17. Davies. TM. 32.
18. Davies. TM. 34.
19. Bromwich. TYP. 94-95.
20. Williams. PKM. 29.
21. Translated by the author.
22. Note that the common Welsh circumflex over the letter 'a' (brân) does not apply when the term is used within the context of a title.

23. https://www.rspb.org.uk/birds-and-wildlife/identifying-birds/corvids-how-to-identify-the-crow-family
24. Bromwich. TYP. 291.
25. Davies. TM. 232.
26. Ford. SCA. 104-105.
27. Parker. FBOTM. P 348-349.
28. Williams. PKM. P 40.
29. Translated by the author from MAW. P 127.
30. Williams. PKM. P44.
31. Williams. PKM. P207-208.
32. Williams. PKM. P 44.
33. Davies. TM. P 32.
34. https://welsh-dictionary.ac.uk/gpc/gpc.html
35. Williams. PKM. P45.
36. https://welsh-dictionary.ac.uk/gpc/gpc.html
37. https://welsh-dictionary.ac.uk/gpc/gpc.html

A Guide to Welsh Pronunciation

A glossary of words can be found at the authors YouTube page – https://www.youtube.com/channel/UCtpV2UP46Avd76h7OSWY4Lw

The stress of any word almost exclusively stands on the penultimate syllable. A vowel is elongated if it appears with a circumflex above it. For example – Don without the circumflex would be pronounced as *Donn*. With the addition of a circumflex –Dôn – would be pronounced *Dawn*.

The Welsh alphabet

a, b, c, ch, d, dd, e, f, ff, g, ng, h, i, l, ll, m, n, o, p, ph, r, rh, s, t, th, u, w, y

Welsh Vowels

a-	Short as in 'mat'	long as in 'farmer'
e-	Short as in 'let'	long as in 'bear'
i-	Short as in 'pit'	long as in 'meet'
o-	Short as in 'lot'	long as in 'lore'
u-	Short as in 'ill'	long as in 'limb'
w-	Short as in 'look'	long as in 'fool'
y-	Short as in 'up'	long as in 'under'

Welsh Consonants

Some may be similar in sound to their English counterparts but with emphasis on heavy aspiration of sound.

b-	as in 'bin'
c-	as in 'cat'
ch-	guttural as in 'loch', never as in 'chin'
d-	as in 'dad'
dd-	as in 'th' sound in 'them' never as in 'thin'

e-	as in 'elephant'
f-	as in 'van'
ff-	as in 'off'
g-	as in 'gate' never as in 'gem'
ng-	as in 'song' never as in 'linger'
h-	as in 'hit', it is never silent
l-	as in 'lit'
ll-	no counterpart, voice by placing tip of tongue in 'L' position and exhaling voicelessly through the sides of the mouth.
m-	as in 'mat'
n-	as in 'nit'
p-	as in 'part'
ph-	as in 'phrase'
r-	is trilled by the tip of the tongue as 'ravioli' in Italian
rh-	no counterpart, voice by placing tongue in 'r' position and exhale quickly and harshly but voicelessly, through the narrow gap the lips form.
s-	as in 'sit' never as in 'kiss'
t-	as in 'tap'
th-	as in 'thick' never as in 'them'

Bibliography

Primary Sources

The White Book of Rhydderch (Llyfr Gwyn Rhydderch), Peniarth Manuscript 4, National Library of Wales.

https://www.library.wales/discover-learn/digital-exhibitions/manuscripts/the-middle-ages/white-book-of-rhydderch

The Book of Taliesin (Llyfr Taliesin), Peniarth Manuscript 2, National Library of Wales.

https://www.library.wales/discover-learn/digital-exhibitions/manuscripts/the-middle-ages/book-of-taliesin

Peniarth Manuscript 131, National Library of Wales.

https://viewer.library.wales/6057827#?xywh=-1382%2C-1%2C5979%2C5020&cv=21

Williams, Ifor (1978) *Pedeir Keinc Y Mabinogi allan o Lyfr Gwyn Rhydderch (PKM),* Cardiff, Wales UP.

Secondary Sources

Bromwich, Rachel. ed. (2014). *Trioedd Ynys Prydein*. Cardiff: University of Wales Press.

Chandler, K. (2002). *Patriarchy and Power in Medieval Welsh Literature*. Proceedings of the Harvard Celtic Colloquium, 22, 80–95. http://www.jstor.org/stable/40285164

Davies, Sioned. (2007). *The Mabinogion*. Oxford University Press.

Eichner, Elaine, S. (2018). *Magical Birds as a link between the Mabinogion and other Celtic literature: Facts and Fancies.* https://repository.uwtsd.ac.uk/id/eprint/1701/1/1701%20Eichner%2C%20Elaine%20%282018%29%20MA%20Magical%20birds.pdf

Elmes, M. R. (2018). *Failed Ritualized Feasts and the Limitations of Community in "Branwen ferch Lŷr."* Proceedings of the

Harvard Celtic Colloquium, 38, 201–215. http://www.jstor.org/stable/45373683

Gire, J. (2014). *How Death Imitates Life: Cultural Influences on Conceptions of Death and Dying*. Online Readings in Psychology and Culture, 6(2). https://doi.org/10.9707/2307-0919.1120

Goldwasser, M. (1994). *What Drives the "Mabinogi?"* Proceedings of the Harvard Celtic Colloquium, 14, 49–57. http://www.jstor.org/stable/20557274

Haycock, Marged. (2015). *Legendary Poems from the Book of Taliesin* (LPBOT). Aberystwyth: CMCS Publications.

Hemming, J. (1998). *Reflections on Rhiannon and the Horse Episodes in "Pwyll."* Western Folklore, 57(1), 19–40. https://doi.org/10.2307/1500247

Ifans, Dafydd, Ifans, Rhiannon. and Roberts, B.F. (2007). *Y Mabinogion: diweddariad*. Llandysul: Gomer.

Kay, M. (2004). *Gendered Postcolonial Discourse in the Mabinogi.* Proceedings of the Harvard Celtic Colloquium, 24/25, 216–228. http://www.jstor.org/stable/40285191

Macana, Proinsias. (1958). *Branwen Daughter of Llŷr*. Cardiff: University of Wales Press.

Moisseeff, Marika. (2020) *Dealing with death in contemporary Western culture: A view from afar.* Jone Salomonsen; Michael Houseman; Sarah M. Pike; Graham Harvey. Reassembling Democracy: Ritual as Cultural Resource, Bloomsbury Academic, pp.179-191, 2020, 9781350123014. 10.5040/9781350123045.ch-010 . halshs-03096279

Owen, Jones; Morganwg, Iolo; Pughe, Owen William. (1870). *The Myvyrian Archaiology of Wales: Collected out of Ancient Manuscripts*. Denbigh: Thomas Gee & Sons.

Parker, Will. (2005). *The Four Branches of the Mabinogi*. Oregon House, Ca: Bardic Press.

Starling, Mhara. (2025). *Pagan Portals: Y Mabinogi: Exploring the Magic and Wisdom of Welsh Mythology*. London: Moon Books.

Sullivan, Charles W. ed. (1996). *The Mabinogi, a book of essays.* New York: Garland Pub.

Telyndru, Jhenah. (2023). *The Ninefold Way of Avalon: Walking the path of the priestess.* Woodbury: Llewellyn Publications.

Thomson, Derick, S. (1976). *Branwen Uerch Lyr.* The Dublin Institute for Advanced Studies.

Tolstoy, Nikolai. (2009). *The Oldest British Prose Literature: The compilation of the Four Branches of the Mabinogi.* Lampeter: The Edwin Mellen Press.

Williams, Mark. (2021). *The Celtic Myths that Shape the Way We Think.* Thames & Hudson.

About the Author

Kristoffer Hughes is founder and head of the Anglesey Druid Order, he is a Druid in the Order of Bards, Ovates and Druids and a Druid member of the Gorsedd of Wales (Gorsedd Cymru). He is an award-winning author of several titles that focus on Welsh mythology, death, dying and bereavement. He worked professionally in service to HM Coroner for 32 years. He is an RTS and BAFTA award winning Welsh language television presenter. He leads workshops and courses online and in person throughout the UK, Europe, the USA and Australia. You can contact him by searching for Kristoffer Hughes on Facebook and at angleseydruidorder.co.uk

You Might Also Like

Pagan Portals – Arianrhod
Celtic Goddess of Fate, Fortune and Destiny

978-1-80341-827-8 (Paperback)
978-1-80341-915-2 (e-book)

Readers of ebooks can buy or view any of these bestsellers by clicking on the live link in the title. Most titles are published in paperback and as an ebook. Paperbacks are available in traditional bookshops. Both print and ebook formats are available online.

Find more titles and sign up to our readers' newsletter
www.collectiveinkbooks.com/paganism

For video content, author interviews and more, please subscribe to our YouTube channel.

MoonBooksPublishing

Follow us on social media for book news, promotions and more:

Facebook: Moon Books

Instagram: @MoonBooksCI

X: @MoonBooksCI

TikTok: @MoonBooksCI